Eighteen Wheels
North to Alaska

A History of Trucking in Alaska

CLIFF BISHOP
Ice Road Trucker

Publication Consultants — Since 1978

PO Box 221974 Anchorage, Alaska 99522-1974
books@publicationconsultants.com—www.publicationconsultants.com

ISBN 978-1-59433-110-7
Library of Congress Catalog Card Number: 2009932627

Front Cover Photo

The cover shows Gene Roggee's 1953 Kenworth, driven by Cliff Bishop, struggling south of Anaktuvuk Pass on the Ice Road to the North Slope.

Manufactured in the United States of America.

Dedication

Eighteen Wheels North to Alaska has been more than ten years in the making and my truck driving stopped at age 85. In the meantime, my wife, Jeanne, and I have sold our oversized house that we worked on and finally finished after about ten years of hard work, and have been working the last couple of years on a small cabin that is nearing completion in the Kasilof area. This will be our retirement home in the Alaska woods. My goal is to put *Eighteen Wheels North to Alaska* into print and attempt through this medium to retain some of the history of trucking in Alaska. *Eighteen Wheels North to Alaska* is dedicated to our early-day trucking pioneers.

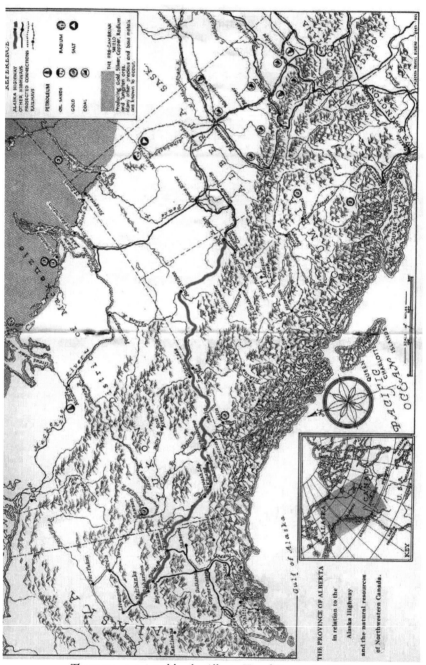

The map was printed by the Alberta Travel Bureau in 1943.

4

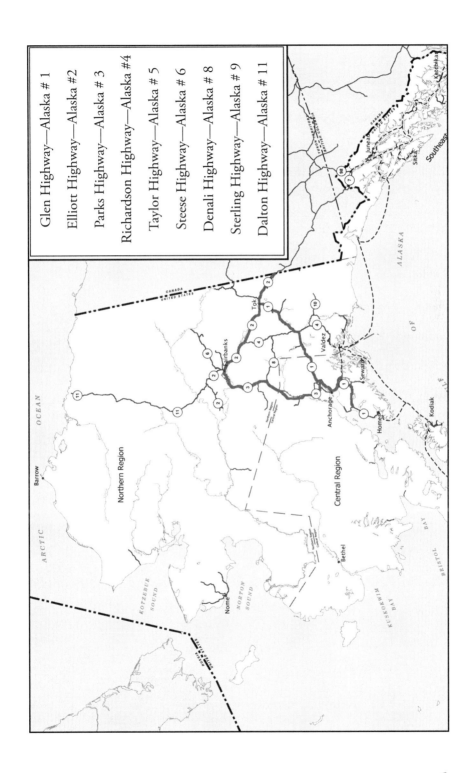

Glen Highway—Alaska # 1

Elliott Highway—Alaska #2

Parks Highway—Alaska # 3

Richardson Highway—Alaska #4

Taylor Highway—Alaska # 5

Steese Highway—Alaska # 6

Denali Highway—Alaska # 8

Sterling Highway—Alaska # 9

Dalton Highway—Alaska # 11

Contents

Acknowledgments

I express my thanks to those who furnished the photos: Alaska Film Archives at the University of Alaska Fairbanks, Dirk Tordoff, director, Don Hill, Bob Hill, Gene Rogge, Fred Hupprich, Mark Moore, and Bob Cavalero. Much gratitude is extended to Gene Rogge, Mark Moore, Fred Hupprich, Eddie O'Leary, and Charley Barr for their help in establishing and confirming names, dates, and places. And, for help from Rebecca Bishop, Russ Barnes, Kim LeBrell, and Jerry Gibson, I extend appreciation for transcribing the manuscript and help with the computer. Without each of your valuable assistance, *Eighteen Wheels* would have never happened.

Alaska's Highway System

Glen Highway—Alaska # 1

The Glenn Highway runs for 328 miles from Anchorage to Tok. The road runs from Anchorage to Glennallen and intersects with the Richardson highway at milepost 115, you then travel 13 miles to the left up the Richardson to Gakona Junction to milepost 128 where you turn off on what is known as the Tok cutoff, but is still designated as the Glenn highway, Alaska. # 1, this road runs for 125 miles to Tok where it intersects with the Alaska Highway.

Elliott Highway—Alaska #2

The Elliott also branches off from Fox and continues for 70 miles to Livengood and then for another 87 miles on to Manley Hot Springs.

Parks Highway—Alaska # 3

The Parks starts from the Glen highway 35 miles north of Anchorage and continues for 323 miles to Fairbanks, when you add the 35 miles on it is a total of 358 miles from Anchorage to Fairbanks. This Highway was known as the Anchorage Fairbanks Highway after completion in 1971, this road is the main route between Anchorage and Fairbanks and runs parallel to the Alaska railroad, it also takes you to the entrance of Denali Park. Most people believe the road is called the Parks because of its route into and past Denali Park, however it is named after George Parks the former territorial governor from 1925 to 1933 .On a clear day you can get a wonderful view of Denali Mountain from the highway on this route.

Next Richardson Highway—Alaska #4

The Richardson runs from Valdez to Fairbanks for a distance of 360 plus miles and is covered within this book from its beginning as a well used horse trail until the Army sent a truck from Valdez to Fairbanks in 1913, this truck made about 50 miles per day on this maiden voyage and opened up the trip to civilian use as witnessed by Bobby Sheldon's trip in the same year in a new Model T Ford Car, by 1920 motorized traffic was fairly common and Gene Rogge in 1929 opened the Richardson up to commercial traffic with His delivering 8 barrels of gasoline from Valdez to Fairbanks.

Taylor Highway—Alaska # 5

The Taylor begins 12 miles south of Tok off of the Alaska Highway at Tetlin Junction and ends 165 miles later at Eagle on the Yukon River, this picturesque journey takes you through the village of Chicken and the historic 40 mile mining district, you connect with what is called the top of the world highway 96 miles in from Tetlin and from this spot known as Jack Wade Junction the road continues on for 76 miles to Dawson City, Yukon Territory where it is possible to continue on to Whitehorse, Y.T. Take a turn to the left at Jack Wade and you are off to Eagle and the Yukon River, another trip that you will not soon forget because of the spectacular scenery.

Steese Highway—Alaska # 6

The Steese extends for 162 miles from Fairbanks to Circle on the Yukon River, this road starts at Fox just out of Fairbanks.

Denali Highway—Alaska # 8

The Denali was completed in 1957 and runs from Paxson on the Richardson to Cantwell on the Parks, there are huge areas visible to the traveler on this road and usually many animals can be seen such as Moose, Caribou and Bear, truly a spectacular stretch of road and a lot to be seen in only 135 miles of travel.

Sterling Highway—Alaska # 9

The Sterling is 142 miles long and was completed in the 1950s, it starts at Tern Lake off of the Seward highway and goes through Cooper Landing,and you are able to ride past beautiful Kenai Lake and also stretches of the Kenai River all of which are breathtaking, you travel on to Soldotna and past the road to Kenai which lies just off the Sterling highway you then continue on down toward Homer, part of the way while motoring alongside Cook Inlet with views of several active Volcanos across the Inlet, next comes Homer and a beautiful panorama of mountains and sea as you top the hill overlooking the town, you continue on down to what is known as the Homer Spit which extends 5 miles out into Kachemak Bay, at this point if you are to continue your travels it is necessary to get on board an Alaska Marine Highway ship to get to Kodiak or turn around and head back inland.

Dalton Highway—Alaska # 11

The Dalton Highway, also known as the Haul Road begins at Livengood and ends at Deadhorse. Coldfoot is at mile 175, Wiseman at mile 188 and Deadhorse at mile 414, the service road continues on to Prudhoe Bay.

Alaska Highway

The Alaska Highway runs from Dawson Creek, British Columbia to Delta Junction, Alaska and enters Alaska near Beaver Creek, Yukon Territory, continues up through Tok, Dot Lake and on to Delta Junction where it officially ends and intersects with the Richardson Highway.

Foreword

I put the stories in this book together from my own experiences and memory; also from stories related to me by other old timers. Although I diligently tried to write everything with total accuracy, as it supposedly happened, I'm certain there will be discrepancies found, so I have to go with the following words I've heard many times from a codriver of mine as we were gathered around with several other truckers B.S.-ing and having coffee. One of them would always come up with a wild tale that everyone knew was a stretch on the truth, if not an outright lie. As usual, one of the truckers would speak up and start to disagree with the story teller when my codriver would say, "leave him alone it's his story, let him tell it the way he wants to." I have to go with that philosophy and apologize for any mistakes you think I may have made; however, it's my story let me tell it the way I want.

Thanks,
Cliff Bishop

Introduction

I was driving down the road on a cold winter night. The moon was full and the skies were totally clear, with mountains standing out in three dimensions, and the lights reflecting off the ice fog that had dropped down on the road. They were sparkling like a million diamonds. I had two cases of oil sitting between the seats, one on top of the other, and I carried a marking pen. And with that marking pen I started writing down a little story as I was going down the road. I was able to make most of it out the next morning and put most of it down on paper, the first and only time I ever wrote anything like it—and a blessing, I guess. It is entitled, *Love Affair*.

It was a strange beginning for a love affair—when I first met her she had already known a lot of lovers and, in fact, had a very large family that had no intention of leaving her. Another thing was her size. By any standards, she was huge, and her profile could not be explained by any other term than coarse and rugged. My first impression of her was not warmth, but rather a definite coldness toward me. But in spite of all these things, from that very first day when my eyes gazed upon her beautiful but rugged features, I knew that I was falling in love, and yes, she has warmed to me on occasion. However, she still has the habit of turning cold toward me in the blink of an eye. So I never really know from one day to the next how she will treat me. I do know for certain that I have fallen deeply in love and that each night as I go to bed with her, I do so in great bliss, and as I awake in the morning and my eyes gaze upon her beautiful, rugged features, I say to her, "Good morning, Alaska, I love you."

Chapter One
Eighteen Wheels North to Alaska

"Ten-four, buddy. Meet me at Rose's Truck Stop Café for a cup of hot coffee. Take the second off-ramp four miles ahead." On any highway USA, a typical greeting between two stateside truckers on their CB radios—a far cry from trucking in the frozen North, where the next stop could be well over a hundred miles away, with nothing in between but more snow and ice plus the occasional moose or caribou.

This is a history of truck transportation in Alaska and the Arctic North, written to chronicle the historic past and the development of the trails and roads, and the men who pioneered the very first trips to open up the regular supply routes we use today. I use the term *open up* with tongue in cheek, because the Far North can still close in and shut you down without a moment's notice. Any trucker who runs here will agree this can be accomplished in many ways: a high wind with snow drifting over the road in such volume as to defy any road-clearing machinery ever made, or a warm Chinook wind that can change temperatures from minus 30 or colder to plus 40 degrees in a matter of hours, leaving the roads so slick that you can't stand up on them, let alone drive. And of course, avalanches capable of shoving a fully loaded truck completely off the road and taking up to several days to clear away.

It is very difficult to point out and name the very first of the pioneers who had the insight and vision to transition from the horses and wagons of the early-day miners to that new-fangled contraption called a truck. One of the first that comes to mind is Sig Wold, who arrived in Alaska in 1920, went to the Kennecott Copper Mine, and started hauling garbage and picking up and disposing of honey buckets (it wasn't honey) for the local businesses. Sig went on to buy out Hoyt Transfer, becoming Sig Wold Transfer, and operated as such until retiring in 1962.

Many more started moving freight back in the days before there was anything even resembling a decent road: Femmer Transfer, Gene Rogge, Howard Bayless, Bud, Dick, and Bob Roberts, Mark Moore, Al Ghezzi, George Sullivan, Leo Schlotfeldt, Bill Miller, Bob McComb, Frank Chapados, Walter Tate, Tony Zimmerman, George Nehrbas, Slim DeLong, Larry Rogge, Bill Montpetit, and many more.

This is a factual history of the pioneers who had the nerve and guts to challenge the near-impossible barriers of rivers, lakes, and frozen tundra that had never before been traveled over and to take trucks and equipment over trails that in the past had seen only dog teams and horse-drawn sleds. It is my desire to give credit to as many of these original pioneers of transportation as I possibly can and apologize to the ones who may be excluded—another reason for putting this into print, since there are very few of us left to preserve as much of this history as possible. We will also look at some of the most unusual equipment, both in concept and size, ever to traverse the Alaska Arctic North. It is a look into the way of life of a longtime trucker who has spent many years in the Far North driving on the Alcan highway and all of Alaska's existing roads, and often on never before traveled ice roads. We will glimpse the many experiences encountered along the way both in trucking and living the Alaska experience.

In the year 1898, the U.S. Army sent a Major Abercrombie to Valdez to head up what was known as the Copper River Expedition, to coincide with the gold rush of 1898. He had a military trail started inland during the summer. This horse trail was completed to the top of Thompson Pass the first year, and was then extended to Eagle, Alaska, a town on the Yukon River, over the next five years. In 1906 the Alaska Road Commission was formed, and Major Wilds Richardson was named the first commissioner. Being a man of vision, he soon recognized the need to have a usable horse trail to the Fairbanks Interior. Using the portion of the trail built by Abercrombie to Eagle, which veered off to the northeast, Richardson continued north to Fairbanks and this route soon became known as the Richardson Trail. It was used immediately for the transportation of mail, passengers, and freight into the Interior. Several companies ran regularly scheduled trips, which took approximately 11 days to complete. Over the next 24 years, thousands of tons of freight and passengers traveled the trail, which hadn't been improved much. A man named Bobby Sheldon made the first continuous motorized trip over this horse trail in 1913 in a brand-new Model T Ford, traveling from Valdez to

Fairbanks. Needless to say, this trip took several days. The U.S. Army in 1913 also sent a truck over this road from Valdez to Fairbanks—not a fast trip, since they averaged only about 50 miles per day. By 1920 motorized vehicles were a common sight on this rough trail.

Gene Rogge, a true pioneer trucker, made the first round trip hauling paying freight from Valdez to Fairbanks in 1929, because the railroad had washed out one of their crossings and they were really short on gasoline in Fairbanks. He received one hundred dollars for his efforts, but proved to all concerned that freight could be transported by motorized equipment. Gene continued in trucking for many, many years throughout Alaska and went on to own and operate Sourdough Trucking Company, one of the oldest trucking companies in the Far North. Sourdough Freight Lines was originally started at Dawson, Yukon Territory in 1898 by a man named Sourdough Ellis. He started his business hauling wood with horse and sleigh and went on for many years, finally trading the horses for Model T Ford trucks and selling out to Ed Herring in 1923. Gene Rogge married Ed Herring's daughter and bought Sourdough Freight Lines from Ed in 1935 and soon after went from 1-ton flatbeds to Kenworths, and entered big-time trucking. Gene sold Sourdough Freight Lines to Leo Schlotfeldt in 1946. Leo is another old-timer here in this country. Sourdough operates to this day. Being run by Leo's sons, it's one of the oldest companies in the state in years of running.

Ed Herring had two daughters; one married Leo Schlotfeldt and the other was married to Gene Rogge, so this company has basically remained in the same family since 1923. These families have been very much involved in the trucking business for many years and the tradition continues with Bill Rogge, Gene's son, who owns his own company called Eggor Trucking—Rogge spelled backward. Gene certainly was one of the original pioneers, and it was a pleasure to have known and worked with him. Gene told me that one time he sat for three full days on this so-called road from Valdez to Fairbanks, the Richardson Trail—the goat trail as most of them called it. After Gene's first trip in 1929, freight continued to be transported over this route, with the motorized equipment slowly but surely replacing the horse and wagons.

Truck traffic increased over the next few years to the extent that it drew the attention of the Alaska Railroad, which up to this time had supplied all of Interior Alaska with freight that arrived into Seward on ships and then was trans-shipped via rail up to Fairbanks. The Alaska Railroad was constructed to develop Interior Alaska, much as it had been used in the Far West. Because Alaska was a territory and not yet a state, the Alaska Road Commission was also under the control of the Department of the Interior.

The Interior department treated the truckers with total disrespect for several years. The Alaska Road Commission was obviously misnamed, for they lobbied against the trucking industry at the territorial capitol in Juneau, attempting to shut down any and all competition to the almighty railroad. It should have been named the Alaska Railroad Commission, since it was very biased, and in the early 1930s established a toll of 9.65 cents per ton on all motorized freight to be collected at the Nenana River Ferry. The whole intent of this tariff was to put a stop to truck freight out of Valdez to Fairbanks. In spite of this 1930s tariff, which cut down profitability tremendously, the truckers still continued to haul freight. They had a running battle with the Feds at the Nenana river crossing. This was not resolved until around World War II, when the army stepped in and insisted that they cut this out, which they finally did. But it was a battle for several years, and it got highly involved between the Feds and truckers. A lot of people were hurt financially because of the Department of the Interior's handling of rail freight versus trucking, both of which they controlled, and very unfairly from the truckers' standpoint.

Bill Tufford of the Odom Company was one of the people involved in truck transportation, which played a major role in the supply of groceries and supplies in the entire state of Alaska, and the following letter from Tufford to Governor Bill Egan illustrates the thorough conspiracy by the railroad against truckers. Bill gave me a copy when I told him I was going to write a book on the history of trucking in Alaska. I certainly enjoyed his observations of the political conspiracy that took place during these early times, and his comments on the age-old battle between truck and rail transportation that continues to this day.

> December 31, 1962
> Dear William;
> I will try and put some sort of story together relative to the past transportation picture in Alaska. Most of this material is from memory and much of it is opinionated. However, for what it is worth, it is yours. I am not an author (which will be self-evident). I cannot spell or punctuate but here you are.
> To put the hind end of this story first, I must remind you that the American people like socialism, otherwise the Alaska Railroad could never exist as it now does. Some of the people who preach otherwise but join in supporting this socialistic bureau are Alaska Freight Lines, Puget Sound Van Lines, Weaver Bros., Alas-

ka Steamship Co., Garrison Fast Freight and many other smaller carriers who ship with the Alaska Railroad.

It is not the purpose of the above statement to upset you or cause a major riot. To understand the A.R.R. and its success through failure one must understand that the American people like socialism. Any time that there is a buck involved they (these people) will collaborate with, join, support, and travel with these socialists.

The original purpose of the Alaska Railroad was to develop interior Alaska. Keeping this in mind the railroad inaugurated this service by assessing the highest rail freight rates in the world.

Perishable food and freeze were shipped into the country at the shipper's risk without refrigeration in summer and very little heat in the winter. The result was a pitiful mess.

During the summer of 1932 or '33 a few hardy souls conceived the idea of meeting Alaska Steamship Co. ships in Valdez and trucking perishable foods to Fairbanks.

The obstacles these early truck freighters encountered defy description. To begin with, the Richardson Highway (Valdez to Fairbanks) was just a sled-and-wagon road winding its way through the coast range over hundreds of miles of swamp and through the continental divide. When the weather was dry the road was barely passable; when it rained the road was tough. There were several unbridged streams which were impassable during either hot or rainy weather. Maintenance was practically nonexistent.

These roads were maintained by an outfit called the Alaska Road Commission. The Alaska Road Commission was a stepchild of the Dept. of Interior, administered at this time by that "Great American" Harold Ickes, a disciple of Russian politics. The Alaska Road Commission personnel, especially the chiefs, consisted of a bunch of pension waiters who were already in semi-retirement. When the Alaska gyps started using the Richardson Highway he constituted a nuisance for Road Commission personnel. The trucker upset the routine and disturbed the siestas of this quietly resting gentry. Some truckers even had the effrontery to make depreciating remarks about the nonexistent efforts of the Alaska Road Commission. It is hard to understand why the Alaska Road Commission people took such an antagonistic attitude toward these truckers until you realize that the A.R.C. was an Interior Department agency, the same department that runs the railroad. The General Manager of the railroad and the head of the A.R. had several meetings a year.

These A.R.C. people worked four months per year, June, July, August, and September. However many of them were paid on a year-around basis. Physical conditions and harassment by the A.R.C. were just too much for these original truckers; they either gave up or went broke.

In 1930 or '31 our Republican friends in Washington passed a bill which was designed to eliminate any form of competition to the railroad. This act imposed a $9.65 a ton toll on all cargo moving up the Richardson Highway to Fairbanks. This act was never enforced though, until Friendly Ickes appeared on the scene.

To further restrain trade and limit competition, the railroad reduced their carload rates during the summer months, when trucks were running from $4.68 per hundred to $2.50 per hundred. As soon as winter came and the Richardson Highway closed for the winter they boosted their grocery rate. They also represent through rates, Seattle to Fairbanks. Other rates remained more or less stable because due to the ocean-measurement-based tariff to Valdez, many commodities that did not come on a weight basis could not be handled by truck.

Alaska Steamship Company delivered to Valdez on what they called a local tariff. They delivered to Seward, for trans-shipment by rail, on a through tariff. The through tariff was predicated on a weight basis, the local tariff on a measurement basis.

It cost more to deliver a carton of toilet paper or corn flakes to Valdez than it did to deliver this same item to Fairbanks via rail. This was a monopolistic, trade-restraining gimmick which along with the toll and the summer price cutting was supposed to eliminate the gypo.

While the original Alaska gypo did give up there was always someone who came along to take his place so, actually, through the early and mid 1930s there were always a few trucks running during the summer months.

When the act was passed creating the Alaska Railroad, it stated, in part, that the railroad would be self-supporting. Since that time the railroad has received appropriations in excess of $25,000,000.00, which it has not repaid. The railroad has sold in the neighborhood of $4,000,000.00 worth of surplus materials which it has received, free of charge, from military agencies in Alaska. Also, a great deal of the installation at Whittier was constructed by the military. In addition to all this free financing the Alaska Railroad does not pay taxes of any kind. Here we have the biggest single business in Alaska, operating in competition with tax-paying private companies, receiving huge handouts from Washington, operating on a tax-free basis and still unable to cut the mustard.

To return again to the truck vs. the railroad, Alaska, during the '30s, let us sum up briefly.

1. We have a bunch of hungry gypos operating over the world's worst road, a distance of 371 miles.

2. These gypos have to operate over this road, which is maintained by the Interior Department, which also operates the competition.

3. The railroad has a trade-restraining price-fixing agreement with Alaska Steamship Co., the only water carrier at this time, whereby the truckers have to pay excessive measurement rates.

4. The Interior Department enforces a discriminating toll against freight coming into Fairbanks which amounts to $9.65 per ton. Remember this toll did not apply to any goods coming up the Richardson Highway except that which came to Fairbanks.

5. In June, when trucks started operating, the railroad reduced rates about 40%. In October, when the roads closed for the winter, rates went up 40%. During all this time the truckers were continually harassed by a bunch of pension waiters whose only claim to fame is that they were retired with pay without ever going to work. An example of this: The A.R.C. enforced a sixteen-thousand-pound gross load limit. This precluded the use of any combination of vehicles and limited a carrier to about a four-ton payload.

Twenty-five years ago the American people still had quite a bit of fight left in them. When the Alaska gypo was squeezed on one hand by a price-fixing, trade-restraining deal between Alaska Steamship and the railroad and on the other hand by discriminating restraining tactics by the railroad and the Alaska Road Commission he, the gypo, fought back; herein lies another tale.

The toll, which has been mentioned above, was collected at a ferry which crossed the Tanana River, at Big Delta, ninety miles southeast of Fairbanks. There was a scale and a ferry landing located on the southeast side of the river. There was a ferry man and a toll collector taking care of this operation. These two pension waiters sat there during the daylight hours awaiting the broken-down gypo about like a buzzard waits for a sick horse to lie down and die. The pleasure these government punks received from sucking the gypo dry was a wondrous thing to behold.

During the summer of 1939 the gypos just ran out of money. The Valdez Dock Co. had supported the truckers, financially, until the Dock Co. could go no further. A day came when some of the operators just did not have the money to pay the toll. One evening three outlaws (government designation for truckers) were stranded on the Valdez side of the river without funds with which to pay the toll. After some discussion these three people came to the conclusion that they were broke, had no chance to survive, nothing to lose, so they decided to borrow the ferry. One gentleman slipped down and removed the chain which guarded the ferry approach. One driver drove his truck onto the ferry (this ferry would only accommodate one truck at a time). While this first trip was being made the resultant noise awakened the toll collector and the ferry operator. These two worthys came charging out of their hole to protect Mr. Ickes' property after a short, swift discussion these two gentlemen were persuaded to return to their den. At this time there was a Toonerville trolley-like telephone line running up the Richardson Highway, from Valdez to Fairbanks. Our two government-employed friends immediately tried to call their Big Brother in Fairbanks. However, when the first truck was unloaded on the Fairbanks side of the river the telephone line became non compos mentis. While this commotion was taking place another taxpayer with a load of freight arrived at the river. Consequently, four gangsters (government designation for taxpayer) moved their trucks across the river and ultimately, that night, streamed into Fairbanks. After this caper, stealing the ferry became a game played by everyone that could rustle up a truck and a load of freight. One character drove the Big Delta, crossed the river, cut a load of wood, hijacked the ferry and returned to Fairbanks. At this time there was wood within ten miles of Fairbanks.

The truckers found strength in numbers; and as resistance to hijacking increased, swarmed down on the ferry in groups.

The bellowing and shrieking from the government pimps constituted one of the most melodious symphonies ever written. Horrible Harold was shooting out a multitude of instructions from Washington. Colonel Olson, the then head of the railroad, had his jaw unhinged and was burping about law and order. Funny when you realize that he headed an illegal, monopolistic, price-fixing, trade-restraining, rate-gouging, socialistic bureau.

The Interior Department was having a little trouble getting what it called law enforcement organized. The Marshall's office was manned by old-time Alaskans who knew what was going on and made a point of looking the other way regarding the toll battle.

The government official who really put on a performance was our now Representative to Congress, Ralph Rivers. Tiger Rivers was then District Attorney of the Fairbanks or Fourth Judicial district, Alaska. Ralphy charged around the courthouse in Fairbanks raising cane with the Marshall's office, making grandiose speeches about law and order, squeaking away about law and order, outlaws and gangsters and, in general, making a horse's ass out of himself which for him wasn't much of a problem.

Doc Gordon was a fellow getting along toward fifty years of age. Doc had been badly crippled in some accident before coming to Alaska, and could walk only with the aid of two canes. Nevertheless, in spite of his condition, old Doc worked alongside of the other truckers, wallowing in the mud and handling freight in an amazing manner.

Doc maintained from the start that the truckers were handling the toll matter incorrectly. Doc felt that the truckers and the government should settle the toll problem in a court of law. Doc had the trucker petition the courts for permission to sue the government and force the government, by court order, to stop collecting the toll which Doc maintained was discriminatory and illegal. The government would not give the truckers permission to sue. Doc then asked the government to sue the truckers for refusing to pay the toll. This the government also refused to do. Doc still felt that there was some lawful way to handle this matter; he refused to steal the ferry, and always paid the toll and attempted to operate in a legal manner.

One day in 1939 Doc Gordon arrived at the Big Delta ferry; his toll charge amounted to about $41.00. Doc only had $37.00 in cash so he asked the toll collector to take his check for $4.00.

The toll collector refused, so Doc offered to leave his fancy watch for collateral until Doc returned from Fairbanks the next day. The collector again refused, so Doc asked to unload part of his freight and leave it for collateral. By this time the toll collector, feeling he had a weak one in old Doc, ran Doc out of the toll shack. Old Doc threw a fit and advised the toll collector, "All of you punks will be sorry that you ever heard of me." After borrowing the $4.00 someplace Doc went on to Fairbanks, parked his truck, begged and borrowed lumber and material, and built a scow. He borrowed a boat to push the scow with and went into competition with the government ferry.

Since the act establishing the toll stated that the toll would be collected at the Big Delta ferry and since the truckers using Doc's ferry were not using the Big Delta ferry, the truckers were no longer violating any law when they crossed the river.

The government punks squealed like a pig stuck under a gate, puffed and huffed about law and order, complained about the poor price-fizzling, trade-restraining, rate-gouging railroad not getting a fair shake, but agreed if the truckers would put the toll money in escrow the government would sue to recover this money (we will discuss this further later).

About the time that Doc was building his scow, an incident took place at the ferry which is pertinent to this story.

Through the efforts of the Interior Department and Mr. Rivers' office the local Marshall was forced to put a Marshall at Big Delta to guard the ferry. Danny Doyle was the name of the deputy Marshall assigned to do this job. Actually Danny was a good fellow.

One day in the summer of 1939 fourteen truckers drove up to the Big Delta ferry. Between them they did not have enough money to get one truck on the ferry. Many of these trucks were loaded with perishables, so it was imperative that they get across the river. An argument ensued in which the Marshall allegedly pointed his gun at one of the freighters. In self-defense the trucker, with help from the other truckers, subdued the Marshall, trussed him up and locked him in the scale house. The freighters then borrowed the ferry, crossed the river, went on to Fairbanks, and about their business. The next day they were all in jail.

Tiger Ralph Rivers really put on a performance. He raced up and down the corridors in the courthouse shouting, "I've got them this time. They've gone too far now; they'll all wind up in the penitentiary." He really squealed and hollered like a hungry hog in a trough.

The trial took place immediately. Among the guests was price-fixing, trade-restraining, rate-gouging Colonel Olson of the Alaska Railroad.

"Mr." Rivers decided to try the culprits one at a time. The trial was short. The defendant testified that he attacked the Marshall in self-defense. The jury walked out and back in and said "not guilty." The judge grumbled, Rambunctious Ralph slobbered some more and the truckers went back to work. By this time Doc Gordon has his scow on the job.

John McGinn, one of Alaska's most able lawyers, represented the truckers in the toll case. He worked for practically nothing, certain that his arguments would prevail. McGinn did a good job going way back into English law and following through up to the present. Old Pratt the Judge had been extremely unhappy with the restraining-the-Marshall decision. Pratt now had the last word. He said in part "Trucks stir up lots of dust which is bad for the tourists. The roads in Alaska belong to the Federal Government and they can do with them as they wish." The Circuit Court upheld Pratt and the Supreme Court refused to review. No doubt the notoriety attendant with the illegal relative to the ferry squabble affected these decisions.

As a result of these decisions the truckers were in tough shape. Much of the escrow money had been borrowed, everyone around Fairbanks feeling that the truckers would win.

During the summer of 1940 military supplies began coming into Fairbanks. This movement increased during the summer of 1941 as air fields and bases were being constructed all over Alaska. The Pension Waiters made a feeble effort to collect the toll on those supplies, which came up the highway, but an army major, in a hurry, showed someone the business end of a gun and the toll became nonexistent.

When the war came and tremendous tonnages for military installations and pipelines started coming into the country the Alaska Railroad fell flat on its face. The military put a port captain in Valdez, hired all the trucks in the country and tried to complement the Railroad's lack of effort with trucks running out of Valdez. At this point the Alaska Road Commission, who were generally inept and only at best in a partially upright position, swooned completely and reclined alongside the Railroad, also face down. There we now see the results of socialism at work.

The military went to work on the railroad. The army smashed through the Alaska Highway and supplemented the Alaska gypo with many trucks. Tonnage moved, construction of Alaska bases progressed and the gypo trucking industry grew into an important, if somewhat unstable, part of the defense effort.

In an effort to straighten out the road program, in Alaska, and at the military's insistence, a military man, Colonel John Noyes was appointed head of the Alaska Road Commission. Under Colonel Noyes, Alaska's present highway system took shape. Noyes had a tough row to hoe. His staff consisted of this same do-nothing group which had for years hindered Alaska's development. Certainly they resented having Noyes elevated over their own little group. The appointment of an outsider threatened the autonomy of this group. While Colonel Noyes accomplished a great deal, his tenure as head of the A.R.C. was for him an unhappy one.

The head of Alaska Freight Lines and one of his swampers met with Colonel Noyes and Angelo Ghiglione, his second in command, to attempt to get permission to maintain the road out of Valdez. Mr. Ghiglione protested, violently, against this plan. Colonel Noyes, who was partially deaf, presented that he did not hear Mr. Ghiglione and went ahead and put a deal together.

Alaska Freight Lines agreed to pay the A.R.C. to keep the approaches to the Valdez Summit open. Alaska Freight Lines agreed to keep the nineteen miles, over the summit, open. The A.R.C. agreed to loan Alaska Freight Lines five tractors to help with this work.

The people of Valdez subscribed money to the project. The Valdez Dock Co. also contributed. Alaska Freight Lines put some snowplows together out of odds and ends. A crew was recruited from the people of Valdez. These people were interested in seeing this project succeed and worked long and hard for a nominal wage. The freight moved through Valdez during the winter of '49 and '50. The project was considered a success.

Winter maintenance of the Valdez Summit spelled the end of the Alaska Railroad's monopoly on general cargo and perishable goods in Interior Alaska. It also stopped the summer-to-winter rate-juggling act that the Railroad had been carrying out for years.

The Railroad still had an ace in the hole, however, to finance their shenanigans.

For many years the Standard Oil of California was the only oil company doing business in Interior Alaska. Their plant in Fairbanks was, and still is, located on Alaska Railroad property. At one time Standard Oil's lease with the Railroad stipulated that the Alaska Railroad would be the sole carrier of bulk petroleum products to Standard Oil's terminal at Fairbanks. Standard Oil furnished the tank care, and still does, paid for the maintenance of these cars and loaded and unloaded the product. The Railroad's rate was $1.20 per hundred, or around nine cents per gallon, Seward to Fairbanks. This rate is much higher than the rate on salt, sugar, groceries, malt liquors, and many other items shipped in carload lots. In recent years this petroleum rate has been slightly reduced but is still much higher than many other carload rates. The Railroad must handle all these dry commodities from ship to rail; they must also deliver these items at destination and stand a certain amount of loss due to damage and theft. Considering the difference in service and the extra handling costs the Railroad is charging about double for bulk petroleum products over other carload shipments. The reasoning behind this is simple. By holding a monopolistic gun over the bulk petroleum users in Interior Alaska the Alaska Railroad is able to extort millions of dollars from the people of Interior Alaska. With this capital the Railroad is able, with appropriations from Congress and with the sale of surplus military equipment to force competent taxpayers out of business. Here we have the workings of a socialistic, monopolistic bureau cheating their customers and competitors while collecting funds from every taxpayer from Maine to California and from Alaska to Florida. Carl Marx would do the twist, in glee, if he could observe this operation.

Many truckers have offered to transport bulk petroleum products from Valdez to Fairbanks for less than the present rail rate.

[In] the defense of the Standard Oil it must be pointed out that they have a large installation at Seward which they operate themselves while their plant in Valdez is small and operated by a consignee. However, Standard Oil publishes a little book telling about their growth with Alaska and about their part in the development of the state. It is doubtful if a trade-restraining, price-fixing agreement which allows the Alaska Railroad to steal millions of dollars from the people of Interior Alaska is developing anything.

Since the Union Oil Co. and Texaco have entered the trade in Alaska. Texaco does not a have a plant there. Union Oil has also resisted all efforts relative to the movement of bulk petroleum products to Fairbanks. Union Oil does have a plant there. Union Oil has also resisted all efforts relative to the movement of bulk petroleum products to Fairbanks. Union Oil's plant in Fairbanks is also located on railroad property.

One Union Oil service station, in Fairbanks, operates its own truck out of Valdez. In order to operate this truck, the people who own this service station also operate a service station at Big Delta. The Big Delta gasoline must come out of Valdez so these people are able to supply their station in Fairbanks. Not, however, with the blessing of the Union Oil Co. This one truck has reduced the service station pump price in Fairbanks from 55 cents per gallon to 48.9 cents per gallon. However, this is no help to bulk petroleum users.

When Alaska Freight Lines attempted to keep the Valdez summit open Colonel Noyes promised that if at all possible and providing that Freight Lines was successful, the Alaska Road Commission would, in the future, maintain this road on a year-around basis. John Noyes left the Alaska Road Commission in 1950 and our friend, Angelo Ghiglione, took his place. This was indeed a sad day for Alaska's highway program. In September of 1950 truckers were advised to get out of Valdez as funds were not available for the winter maintenance of the Valdez summit. The truckers questioned this statement because the defense department had requested Congress to include such funds in the A.R.C. appropriation. A little sleuthing turned up the fact that Colonel Johnson, then General Manager of the Railroad, and Honorable Ghiglione had taken a trip down the Tanana and Yukon rivers on one of Alaska Railroad's boats. Humped over a case of good Scotch (purchased by the American taxpayer) these two worthies decided to write the Alaskan trucker off, hence the notice to vacate Valdez. By closing the Richardson the Railroad would again be without competition. Alaska Freight Lines took the problem directly to Washington. This problem was presented to Henry Jackson, Senator from the State of Washington; Jackson represented the people of Alaska before Senate sub-committee. Jackson questioned pension waiter Ghiglione. The questions were searching and factual. Ghiglione sneaked off, tail between his legs, and the Road Commission maintained the road. Strange as it may seem, the job was done without further appropriations. The money which had not been available showed up in the till....

At the time the Alaska Railroad came into existence there was a small but busy marine operation on the lower Yukon. These small carriers picked up freight from steamships at the mouth of the Yukon and transported this cargo up the Yukon into the Tanana and Koyukuk rivers. One of the Railroad's first jobs was to run these taxpayers out of business. The Railroad hauled cargo 400 miles up the Railroad from Seward and then hauled it backward eleven hundred miles to the mouth of the river. The cost to the customer at the mouth of the river was the same as it was landed at Nenana. The Railroad hauled freight eleven hundred miles for nothing just to break a few tax-paying river freighters. Eventually, after all the taxpayers freighting on the river were defunct, the Railroad leased their equipment and retired from river transportation.

In 1953 or '54 Garrison Fast Freight showed the Railroad how to transport a cabbage without cooking it or freezing it to death. This led to piggy-backing of all cargo at unpublished rates. Some carriers got better rates than others. Regulations were more restrictive on some carriers than others and schedules were regulated to favor certain connecting characters.

There was never any outfit in the world that manipulated rates and made under-the-table deals to compare with the shenanigans of the Alaska Railroad; example: the railroad transports cargo from Seward to the military bases near Anchorage, a distance of more than a hundred miles, for the same price it hauls this same cargo from Anchorage to these same bases, a distance of five miles or less.

As Alaska grew, so did its regulatory boards and bureaus. Under Statehood we find that Alaska has a definitely unfriendly attitude toward highway truckers. At the present time all the roads that parallel the Alaska Railroad are restricted for overweight permit loads. Alaska has the highest fuel tax of any state in the nation. Many of Alaska's roads are not considered as part-time operators, but are taxed as if they were operating on a year-round basis. The largest operator of trucks in the state is the Alaska Railroad; they do not pay taxes of any kind.

For many years employees of the Alaska Road Commission, a Federal agency, lobbied against the trucking industry in the Territorial Capital in Juneau.

The Alaska Road Commission, with divine guidance from above, pooped away the better part of two hundred million dollars. To show for this we have a bunch of 20-foot roads so rough that they make the Coney Island Roller Coaster look as smooth as a mill pond.

It will take the state forever to rectify the mistakes created by the Alaska Road Commission. All the roads the A.R.C. ever built will have to be, eventually, relocated. By the time this is finished taxes and licenses will be so expensive that an individual will be fortunate to be able to operate a bicycle.

Goodbye. (end of letter)

Chapter Two
In the Beginning

After the military shut the toll thing off at Nenana, they built a bridge over the river and it did totally away with the ferry. With the toll removed and construction going full bore up in the Interior, the flood of freight began moving out of Valdez, with a loaded truck leaving every 15 minutes for its Interior destination. This continued to well up through the war years, and with the end of World War II the demand of such volumes of freight slowed down. The next segment we'll approach is the Alcan highway, starting in 1942 in the war years.

On December 7, 1941, when the Japanese attacked Pearl Harbor and involved the United States in World War II, some of our brighter military minds knew immediately that we needed a connection between the South 48 and Alaska, for military purposes for the defense of the whole northern hemisphere. So they opted to build this road, this Alcan, starting from Dawson Creek and ending up in Fairbanks, Alaska, for a distance of around 1,500 miles. Over 20,000 civilians and army soldiers completed this road. They started in March 1942, and completed it in November 1942, a period of nine months. It was truly one of the more miraculous things ever, and it was amazing that it could be done, but they did indeed and finished the job. Although it was not a great road, it was traversable by motorized equipment, and the army immediately started hauling military trucks and equipment over this highway.

In the early part of 1943, shortly after the Alcan opened to military traffic, three civilians were given special permission to haul telephone line equipment from Dawson Creek, B.C., to Whitehorse Y.T. These early-day pioneers were Bob McComb, Walter Tate, and Tony Zimmerman. They left from Fairbanks, and it took them 12 days to complete the trip south to Dawson Creek on the first leg of this epic journey. After a short rest they loaded up and headed back north. There were no bridges over the rivers at that time, so all of the crossings were done on the river ice. It was a precarious undertaking and Bob said it would take a whole book to cover the incidents that occurred on this trip, the tire problems, getting stuck numerous times, mechanical breakdowns with no services at all anywhere on the road. In spite of everything, they completed the trip in 30 days' time, taking 18 days on the trip north to Whitehorse. This round trip can be made in less than four days with today's equipment, with one rig carrying more weight than all three trucks put together, including their loads.

No more civilian loads were hauled until 1946, when a massive maritime strike on the west coast effectively shut down all water freight coming into Seward that connected with the Alaska Railroad. This had an immediate effect on supplies of all kinds throughout the entire state. The truckers, as usual, when they saw this opportunity, approached it head-on. Several of these pioneer truckers started hauling over this rough, graveled road from Seattle to Alaska, facing the challenges of the trip—and they were many and varied. Those that didn't blow up their engines, transmissions, or rear ends, or turned over, made the trip.

They had to go to Great Falls, Montana at that time to reach Edmonton, Alberta and then proceed to Dawson Creek, B.C. in order to reach the start of the Alaska Highway. There were no bridges across the Smith, Smokey, and Peace Rivers between Edmonton and Dawson Creek, B.C. Ice crossings had to be negotiated or the trucks had to be hauled across the rivers by rail—the latter was very difficult because of the lack of loading ramps and a shortage of flatcars of the proper length.

It wasn't until 1952 that the Hart Highway was opened from Prince George to Dawson Creek. When that road opened it made the trip to Alaska 500 miles shorter, which was a great blessing for these early-day truckers. Al Herda, Jim Booky, Al Ghezzi, Ray DeGross, Dean Hart, and Robert Downs were some of the early-day truckers, along with an Alaska company, Anchorage Cold Storage (ANCO), and others who were optimistic that they could deliver freight on a regular schedule over this route. Although their schedules were often disrupted by weather, road closures, mechanical breakdowns, and other unforeseen circumstances, they never backed off.

With their pioneering travel, freight has continued from that time to the present with fresh fruits, vegetables, and merchandise of all descriptions be-

ing delivered both north and south in less than three days' time in and out of
Seattle. Al Herda, operating as Herda Alaska Truck Lines, started hauling out
of Minneapolis and, as I understand, further down the road he aligned with
Jim Booky, who later was involved with Lynden Transfer. They hauled on a
joint venture north up the Alcan through Canada to Alaska.

Another of the many stories of the trials and tribulations of the early-day
truckers was that of Robert Downs, one of the original pioneers of the Alcan
Highway. He operated as AR-DEES Alaska and was hauling milk from the
South 48 into Alaska. I recall that on one of the trips his driver was making
up there, he spun out on a hill and slid backward down the hill and back over
the bank, wrecking the whole load of milk. About a week later, another one of
his trucks was up there and it also got into trouble and spilled its load. When
Robert Downs talked to the driver over the phone when they finally made
a connection, Downs asked him where he had wrecked, and the driver said,
"Exactly in the same spot as the other one. I went up the hill and slid backward. I went into the same hole that he went into." And Robert Downs said,
"At that rate, if you guys keep doing that, you'll have the hole filled up pretty
soon." I guess it helped to have a little sense of humor about these incidents
even if it didn't help the pocketbook.

Freight increased to a large degree each year after 1947 and trucking out of
Seattle and the Midwest enjoyed a period of good profits. With the road being improved each year, it looked like a long-term situation for the trucking
industry. Then came SeaLand with their huge oceangoing vessels, followed
by Tote with their roll-on, roll-off service for trailers, and between the two
they very effectively shut off Alcan trucking. In the 1990s ocean freight rates
increased, allowing trucks to be competitive, and each year since, more and
more freight has been shipped over the Alcan. The long term is in doubt,
however. With the tremendous increases in fuel prices it remains to be seen if
trucking will continue in such large volumes.

Chapter Three
Alaska Freight Lines

Alaska Freight Lines was started by Al Ghezzi, Bill Miller, Slim Delong, and Tom Donahue, along with Gene and Larry Rogge, in March 1943. This venture lasted about a year with these owners and the equipment was sold out in 1944. Al Ghezzi came back the following year and started operating the Alaska Freight Lines on his own, and it went on to become one of the largest trucking operations Alaska had ever seen. He used equipment never before or since seen in the Far North, hauling ore out of Interior Alaska and freight over the Alcan Highway for several years, and ran many other freighting operations both in Alaska and in the Arctic on the ice roads. If there were a Hall of Fame for truckers, certainly Al Ghezzi would be one of the charter members of it along with Mark Moore, John Clark, Howard Bayless, Gene Rogge, and on and on. They are many and varied—and what I am trying to do is give these people credit for the unbelievable contributions they have made to develop Alaska and the Arctic North.

Alaska Freight Lines was owned by Mr. Al Ghezzi, a true pioneer and innovator of moving freight in Alaska and the Arctic. Having been involved in Alcan hauling, he decided to try another approach and contracted in 1948 to have shipments come up to Haines by sea, and from Haines up to Fairbanks by truck, a distance of 600 miles. The Haines road connecting to the Alcan was not maintained in the winter months, so he could operate only in the summer. So Ghezzi contracted for the barge service to continue farther north into Valdez, thereby cutting the trucking to approximately half the distance, about 300 miles, half the distance from Haines. The big drawback was Thompson Pass, located just inland from Valdez, for it had a tremendous snowfall, and the Richardson Highway had never been kept open there in the winter months because of it. No one, even the old-timers, believed that it was possible to do so, except Ghezzi and some of his top hands. So in the winter of 1949–1950, the Alaska Freight Lines supplied their own snow-moving equipment, and John Clark, who headed up this small crew, moved up to the top of Thompson Pass, lived there all winter, and successfully kept the pass open, thereby creating a year-round supply route to Interior Alaska.

Alaska has had a very short history relating to truck transportation. Most of today's roads were not even in existence until after World War II; therefore, there are still a few of us left who can personally relate to the building of today's road system, as compared to the South 48, where our grandfathers and great-great-grandfathers were the pioneers. The military wanted more than the one route from Seward open, and they were definitely in favor of the truckers having the Richardson road open. In World War II they had these 1½-ton trucks that hauled about eight tons of payload, and they were leaving every fifteen minutes out of Valdez, around the clock, hauling this much-needed freight for the bases that were being constructed in the Interior, at Fairbanks, North Pole, and Northway.

Thanks to Ghezzi they were able to continue year-round operations after he proved that it was possible to keep the pass open throughout the winter months. This operation continued until 1952, when the Seward Highway was completed to Anchorage. This had an immediate effect on the flow of freight—although the freight didn't stop coming into Valdez completely, it definitely slowed way down.

From the very first beginning of transportation of freight in Alaska to the prospectors, the miners, the military and so forth, the roads have never been a barrier, for there have always been those pioneers who have had the courage and conviction that the job could be done. They would take off cross-country with their horse-drawn sleds and wagons to challenge the rivers, ice fields, tundra, subzero temperatures, snowstorms, and countless other challenges.

Chapter Four
Trek to the Arctic Ocean

Al Ghezzi took on one of the biggest jobs ever undertaken with the movement of freight for the construction of the DEW line, the distant early-warning radar system on the Arctic Ocean. This was a high-priority na-

tional defense program to install a system of radar to give the United States early warning of a potential air attack by the Russians. We were involved in a precarious situation with a very real threat of armed conflict. It was a

Bill Unfer and his Peterbilt, the only Peterbilt to make the trip.

The scout plane; a Cessna 180.

The Wein support plane.

Air support.

Bob Cavalero on right with unidentified others.

Hard to keep the coffee cup from spilling.

Well used rigs.

Equipment check.

Ready to roll north.

Rolling north.

Snow Train.

Roll out the barrels.

job that had the very liberty of our country at stake. The same man who had challenged the Richardson Highway and Thompson Pass, Al Ghezzi, came up with a plan to take off cross-country just as those early-day pioneers had with their horse-drawn freight. Ghezzi submitted a plan to the military to move 500 tons of freight for 400 miles across Interior Alaska through a territory where not even dogsleds had been. And to accomplish this seemingly impossible task, he ordered a huge snow train built by the R.G. LeTourneau Company, consisting of the power unit powered by two 400 hp diesel engines that operated 150 KW, DC in line generators that drove 24 electric powered wheels, with power steering front axel and 2,100 gallons fuel capacity pulling five trailers. Each trailer was 16 feet wide and 40 feet long, making the train more than 250 feet in length and capable of carrying more than 150 tons of freight on this trip. In addition, they used 32 conventional diesel trucks and trailers. The military gave final approval for this plan and with the approval all that was left to do was to strike out across never before traveled country, making his own roads using Caterpillar bulldozers. And Al had written into his contract a proposal that if he failed to get the job done overland, he guaranteed that he would fly all the supplies in at no extra cost.

When this project actually got underway, five big D-8 Caterpillars were put on the trail at Circle City in January 1955 where they started the remaining 400-plus mile road to the Arctic coast. In February, seven more Cats followed, widening the road to allow the big 16-foot-wide Snowtrain to follow. This task was completed in 39 days. They sent an Alaska guide and an Indian guide from Fort Yukon ahead of this operation on snowshoes to lead the Cat breaking trail and working in tandem with the following Cats widening the trail. The guides kept in constant contact with each other by radio telephones, with the company plane flying overhead dropping bright-colored stakes that were weighted on one end so they would land in the snow in an upright position, so the guides could follow them and not get off course. These guides would then take the best path in the general direction of the stakes and leave trail markings for the lead Cats to follow. This massive undertaking got underway in the fall of 1954, leaving Fairbanks by the Steese Highway. This was the first time that the Steese was opened in the winter to motorized travel. They proceeded to Chatanika, 17 miles out, and then to Circle Hot Springs, 127 miles up the trail. Next they went to Circle, 153 miles from Fairbanks, where the big snow train was assembled after being trucked in piece by piece. This project was overseen by a man from the LeTourneau factory and the work was done by freight line personnel. They then continued, with their route of travel taking them across the Yukon and on to the Porcupine River area, then to the Coleen River bench, on to Mallard Springs, Old Crow Flats, and through the Blow River Pass, and finally to Shingle Point on the edge of the Arctic Ocean—an easy enough task to put down on paper. It was something else, however, to actually make this unbelievable journey with the plane and guides leading the way. They used this method of navigation all the way to the Arctic Ocean. The plane, a Cessna 180, was piloted by Don Gilbertson, Holly Evans, Bill Lavery, and in addition to the trail-marking detail they kept a constant line of communication open between the frontrunners and the following convoy, carried supplies, and acted as an airborne ambulance when the need arose. They continued day by day for more than 400 miles across the desolate and forbidding territory.

A couple of weeks after this trail-blazing first group left Fairbanks, a team of bulldozers took off, putting the finishing touches on the trail. This unit was actually building the Arctic Highway, the 25-foot-wide road across the roughest, coldest territory in northern Alaska and the Northwestern Territories of Canada. The operation contin-ued 24 hours a day with the big snow train and the tractor truck

Many Cat hours to make this ice cut.

trailers operating behind them and temperatures getting down to close to 70 degrees below zero. The huge snow train and the conventional trucks completed this trip to the Arctic Ocean. Next, the trucks headed back to Eagle on the Yukon River in the early part of 1955, and the snow train was left to be returned to Eagle after freeze-up in late 1955. Bob Cavalero added another interesting piece of information about the Ghezzi DEW line trip: that the Russian radio was broadcasting daily the whereabouts of their first convoy going north. They kept track of the convoy by flying over in their long-range bombers. The Russians have never been bashful about doing flyovers in Alaska.

They had to keep the engines running 24 hours a day to keep from freez-ing up, and they hit heavy, heavy snowdrifts. At times it took several Cats working together to clear these snowdrifts, and it took several hours at times to do this. The bulldozers worked full-time to keep the road going ahead of

Hey! This truck is wider than the road.

Big Mack on the way to the arctic.

What do you think? Is this a good time to ask for a raise?

More than a flat tire.

Is this a crap game or a repair session.

Repairing equipment along the road—in the road.

this convoy and it was very rough going. Often they made only two or three miles a day, and the best they probably ever got was a little more than 20 miles in a single day. We don't have a complete list of the drivers involved in these convoys, but on that list were Vic and Bill Unfer, Bob Cavalero, "Pretty Boy" Ed Smith, Don Stater, Hugh Conners, Lyle Johnston, Ed Montgomery, Glenn Starn, James Booky, Pard Richards, Fred Hupprich, Wilbur Weeks, George O'Leary, Les Seavers, Andy Anderson, Les Crump, Frank (Shifty Harris) Harris (the cook), Don Stoddard (master mechanic), Paul Chamberland, Buck Bradbury, Bob Hill, Jim Rasley, Hambone Johnson, Eddie O'leary, John Clark, Allen Steel, Tom and Jerry Cole, Mark Moore, and Mark's brother-in-law Tony (I don't remember his last name), Forest Wright (the pilot), Glen Starnes, Earl McClure, Andy Warwick, Roger Harris, and his son Keith. These drivers were getting paid $3.75 an hour and were run-

Unloaded and ready to pull truck and trailer out of the ice hole.. A nice day, about zero degrees.

ning about 15 hours a day. After about 15 hours of driving and contending with all the problems that arose, mechanical and so on, they had to fuel up their rigs, check everything out, and get them ready for the following day's operation. Bob Cavalero told me that one of their favorite sayings after crawling into bed for three or four hours and then getting up and going again, was that it sure didn't take long to spend the night here. There was probably more truth than poetry in that statement.

They continued through hundreds of miles of these hills, lakes, and tundra, breaking through ice and having to pull the rigs out with the Cats that were building the road. It's a task almost beyond one's imagination, to keep these rigs underway and repair the various mechanical problems they encountered along the way. And the equipment they were using was a far cry from what is available today. These rigs were operated by men who had experience in operating in arctic conditions and who had a grim determination to get the job done—and get it done they did. They were truly pioneers of the great Arctic Far North, and I feel it's a great privilege to have known or worked with most of them on other jobs and ice-road trips into the Arctic. The equipment was finally brought back near the Yukon River at Eagle, Alaska, after the successful delivery of freight taken out of Fairbanks on the first trip in the winter of 1954 and 1955. In the fall of '55 and winter of '56 they went up the Taylor Highway and supplied this new convoy to take off out of Eagle on the Yukon River. They brought in the big Mack trucks from Valdez, which in itself was a distance of nearly 500 miles over

some very steep and narrow mountain roads. The big Macks pulled trailers that were 12 feet wide and 60 feet long, with a storage capacity of more than 5,500 gallons of fuel in the beds of these huge rigs. They were powered by 600 hp Cummins engines; the loads they carried weighed up to 100 tons, and on top of that the fuel in the trailer beds weighed an additional 40-plus thousand pounds, making a grand total of more than 300,000 pounds gross, with the weight of the truck and trailer thrown in. They were so heavy that Bob Cavalero told me that when they got stuck and put a Cat or two onto them to pull them out, they occasionally broke an inch-and-a-half cable. They reloaded it out of Eagle on the trail north, and after traveling only a short distance it jackknifed and burned. The Macks had a lot of problems with their axles. They had to trade them out, eventually trading out almost all the axles because of problems of

Eskimo families.

breaking. The steel they used was not compatible with the temperatures and became very brittle in the extreme cold. This convoy also carried with them a bunkhouse that slept 16, with a shower and toilet, also a toolshed and workshop.

They refilled all their storage tanks at Norman Wells, where a refinery was located, and then continued toward the Arctic Ocean. They had to build ice bridges over two large rivers on this trip; the Mackenzie River was the largest, a good ¾ miles wide where they crossed it. This was done by pumping water onto the ice and building it up to a thickness of approximately 4 feet and a width of 60 feet. With this much buildup it was capable of supporting all these heavily loaded rigs without a problem. One of the big calamities of this trip was that the big Snow Train with five trailers behind the locomotive caught fire and burned beyond repair, and totally destroyed the generating engines and equipment, thereby putting this whole big train out of commission. They offloaded the five trailers onto Cat trains and proceeded in that manner. They went on to Great Bear Lake, one of the largest lakes in the world, and drove more than 150 miles on it. After getting off this huge lake they took a northeast course toward the Coppermine River, where another one of the troublesome axles broke within 50 miles of Great

Compare the size of man vs Snow Train.   *Little pickup, big Snow Train.*

Bear, and they had to wait for several days for a replacement to be flown in. They finally got everything up and running and continued to the Arctic Ocean, where they met up with an Eskimo with a dogsled and a load of seals he had caught. They knew then that they were getting very close to the Arctic Ocean. He was headed back to his village at Coppermine. They met several other Eskimos who were also carrying seals on their sleds. These Eskimos subsisted on seal and fish; they searched for breathing holes in the ice and when they found one they built a snow house over it, much like an igloo, and then waited for the seal to surface and hooked it. They took the whole seal back to the village, where the skin was removed and used for parkas and other clothing. The rest of the seal was used for the meat. It was quite a sight for the truckers to observe these Eskimos and their lifestyle.

They had gone only 35 miles out on the Coronation Gulf when the lead truck broke through the ice and ended up with all the wheels completely submerged and the trailer bed flat on the surface of the ice. They were very fortunate not to have gone completely under, since it was 700 feet to the

Eskimo families met along the way.

Eskimo sled dog team on the ice.

Eskimo sled dog team on the ice with seal.

Mile and miles of ice and snow.

Running along side the Coronation Gulf.

Thirty-five miles from shore on the Coronation Gulf and the rig breaks through the ice. There is 750 of water under the truck. Unloading the cargo to bob sleds saved the truck and lowboy.

Trying to keep up with the trucks.   *No end in sight.*

Checking the ice on the river.

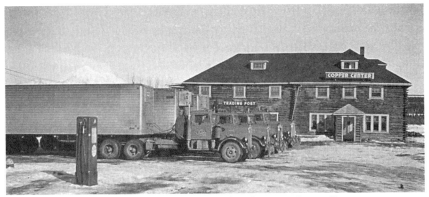

The old Copper Center Hotel with rigs ready to roll.

Drivers ready to depart to the arctic from the Copper Center Hotel.

Lots of hills, snow, and ice.

bottom. This rig was being driven by Roger Harris' son Keith, who was 18 at the time. I can only imagine that he got quite a charge out of that experience. At that point they did not proceed any further on the ocean ice, for it was much too dangerous with such heavy loads, and they were offloaded onto Cat trains and delivered to their final destination in that manner. The original destination for this particular convoy was Victoria Island, and when they broke through the ice they were about 60 miles short of their destination. There were several different convoys and Cat trains and some of the other destinations were Inuvik, Tuktyuktuk, Barter Island, and other Arctic coastal areas.

Another part of their operation was about 50 miles ahead of them: the lead Cat train, which they contacted by radio. After these Cats unloaded their freight they came back, were able to offload the freight, and eventually got the truck removed from the ice without losing any load or equipment. Then they proceeded to offload all the other big loads onto the Cat trains; the Cats then delivered these loads safely to their destinations. Because of the extra trips the Cats had to make, they had taken all the extra fuel off the trucks and the trucks ran out of fuel within 100 miles after leaving the Gulf. So they built a landing strip, and a week or so later a Wien Alaska plane came in, picked up the crew, and flew them back to Alaska, leaving Bob Hill there to wait for the next northbound convoy to refuel the equipment. Drivers from the next convoy were later shuttled back to get these trucks. Part of this equipment was also shipped down the Hay River after the completion of the hauling. This was done after spring breakup; it finally ended up in Edmonton, Alberta. Other equipment was loaded on barges at the Hay River and shipped back to Seattle. The remaining truckers with their food supplies, fuel, and support Cats battled their way back to the Yukon River and Alaska.

Bob Cavalero told me that on the Black Stone River coming back from this second trip, Hambone Johnson ran the Cat down into the river with water up over his lap, and pushed gravel up from the bottom of the river to make an escape ramp to get the rigs back up over the banks. Les Seavers tempered a spring by putting it over an open pit fire and it worked very successfully. Whatever arose on these trips was met head-on by these pioneers on this epic journey, and in all cases they were able to prevail.

Four of the big Mack trucks were retrofitted and shipped back to Alaska and sold to Usibelli Coal Mine at Healy, Alaska, at a later date. These convoys had traveled east on such trips far enough to have been almost due north of Michigan—that's a long ways east from Fairbanks and Eagle, Alaska.

Repairing equipment along the road.

Five miles south of Eagle, 45 degrees below, and warming up the truck to resume trip.

Preheating engine on a very cold morning.

Broken axel 100 miles inland from the gulf.

This was a familiar sight on the 1,900 miles from the Yukon River to the Coronation Gulf.

The results of a little driving error.

Bulldog Mack with Bob Hill and Jim Rasley.

Big switchback. on the road leading to the valley below.

Just one of the many steep hills.

And I thought I was on solid ground.

Andy Anderson with a load of fuel.

At the cook shack: Andy Anderson, Paul Chamberland, Buck Bradbury, and ?.

Missed the road again.

Crossing the Blackstone River Valley.

Getting ready to cross the ice on lake.

Still with the trailer a long way from the ocean.

Nearing their destination.

On the arctic coast.

Big Mack on the way to the arctic.

Arctic winter scene.

One good pull deserves another.

Snow Train.

Bob Hill and Euclid dump truck.

A truck load of fuel.

*Cook shack, mechanic shop,
and sleeping quarters.*

Wrecked Snow Train.

Getting a haircut.

Cats at work.

A group of drivers pose for a photograph.

Snow Train tracks through the snow.

Miles of snow to clear.

Tough going.

Sometimes it doubtful they'll make it.

A hard climb pushing snow.

Getting water from an ice covered river.

Water over ice.

An unidentified driver heading north.

Cats at work pushing snow.

Poor visibility.

Drivers planning the next move.

Heavy duty snow removal.

Air force fly over.

Hugh Schockly

Unloading Cat from the lowboy at 70 below.

Support shacks towed by the Cat.

It's good to let go of the wheel.

Aerial views of the Snow Train's route.

Snow Train control panel

Going home.

Shave and a haircut, how much?

Bob Hill.

Bob Hill.

Mukluk Freight driver.

Snow train on a canyon edge.

George Sullivan visiting with
an unidentified guest.

Convoying north.

Down hill grade leaving Eagle, Alaska.

Talking shop.

Steady, but slow.

Heavy duty snow removal.

Let's go.

Ready to roll north.

Far north grizzly.

Arctic wolf.

Gentlemen. Start your engines.

The drivers and their rigs.

Clearing the drop site.

Chow time.

We began to ask; is there any end to it?

Single cab tractor.

Down again.

Heavy duty trailer.

Taking on water.

Arctic fox.

Still rolling north

Another tragic thing occurred. The plane they used on this second trip was piloted by a young man named Forest Wright, nicknamed "Punk." The plane was a World War II observation plane, and Punk had a passenger with him. They hit an extreme downdraft, and the passenger, named Andy Warwick, was riding in the back seat, sitting on the wing and cowl covers used to keep the plane protected from ice and snow when tied down. Andy couldn't put his seat belt on and was thrown out the back observation window. The suction pulled the wing covers out; they tangled up in the elevators and rudder and caused the plane to crash. The aftermath of this was that Al Ghezzi shut everything down for a couple of weeks searching for them at a huge cost in time and money but they were not found until after spring thaw. Ghezzi never considered anything other than trying to find the flyers regardless of the cost, but again, that is the code of the North and you have to admire it .The burned equipment, the locomotive part of the big, massive snow train, and the five trailers were finally pulled back across the Yukon River and left in a place called Boundary, on the Alaska-Canada boundary there out of Dawson., Y.T. They had been pulled there by Canadian operators using Cats.

I firmly believe that the foregoing historical and factual saga could and should be made into a movie; or at least a documentary of this epic journey. In my opinion it stands with all of the stories of prior trips made by explorers and fortune seekers to the Arctic in years past—only on a much larger scale—and with equipment never seen before or since.

Chapter Five
Snow Train Retrieval

I took a contract to move the power unit and five trailers down the Taylor Highway to the Alcan Highway. A man by the name of John Bridgers was heading up the midwinter recovery operation of a huge snow train. When we arrived at Boundary, the temperatures were in the minus 50s, and from the first day it continued to get colder, dipping into the low minus 60s. This made it necessary to leave the Cat and all the six dump trucks running 24 hours per day. The operation took almost two weeks and the equipment was never shut off from start to finish. The plan was to pull each unit from Boundary down

Two views of the burned Snow Train at Tok.

to the bottom of the hill with the dump trucks, and tow them to where there were bridges over several streams. At that point I would pull each of them across the streams and rivers, since they were much wider than any of the bridges, and after crossing these streams again hook up to the dump trucks and proceed to the next bridge and repeat this operation.

All these plans seemed rather simple and easy; however, it turned out to be a real challenge from the very start. Pulling these huge units down the first hill proved to be impossible for the trucks, for the very first one to start down the hill was nearly pushed off the road by the force of this massive trailer. So I had to hook up to each of these units with the Cat. When I hooked onto the first trailer and looked back over my shoulder I had the feeling that maybe this was going to be a much bigger challenge than I had thought, for the decks of these units were at least 9 feet above the ground and they were very heavy. On these ice-covered roads they had a nasty habit of locking up the wheels because of all the drive gears in each wheel, which were designed for being driven by electric power and not to be towed. With the wheels locking up, the trailer would start to jackknife, threatening to put the whole outfit into the canyon below.

Size of the trailer compared to a truck.

I finally got the first one down to the bottom and that was all I wanted for one day. I loaded the Cat on the lowboy and hauled it back up the hill to Boundary. The next morning I fired up the welder and welded grousers onto the Cat tracks for better traction. It worked very well and I had no more problems keeping the Cat from sliding sideways. After several days I got all the units down the hill, where we hooked up the first truck, but were unable to get it moving even though it was on flat ground. With the low temperatures and the ice, the truck simply did not have enough traction to pull the trailer. After cussing and discussing the situation we all went back down to Bob McComb's Forty-Mile Roadhouse and tried to figure out some way of getting enough weight on the trucks to allow traction.

With such low temperatures everything was like concrete, and the only thing we could come up with was to go back to Fairbanks and load gravel or scrap iron into the dump beds. This was a trip of several hundred miles. We finally gave up and went to bed. I suddenly got an idea of how to fix the problem. I got up in the morning and at breakfast suggested that we borrow a water pump from Bob McComb, drive the trucks down to the Forty-Mile River, put a hole through the ice, and pump water into the dump beds for weight. We put newspaper around the inside of the tailgates and splashed water on the paper, making a perfect seal as it froze instantly, holding the water inside to freeze into a massive block of ice with ample weight to get the job done.

By the time the day was over we had six trucks loaded and ready to go. With all the trucks hooked up to the equipment, we started down the road toward the Alaska Highway and soon came to one of the narrow bridges that required us to go off-road and create a crossing by building

End of the trail for the Snow Train.

a ramp down into the river and up the other side back to the road. This proved to be a real challenge, because at temperatures near minus 60 it is virtually impossible to find any material available to push with the Cat to make these ramps. I therefore backed the Cat to the edge of the riverbank, and with tracks turning I alternated each track by pulling the release levers, keeping the Cat in the same relative position, churning up enough dirt to start a ramp and also break the bank down. I did this on each side of the streams and then dropped way back away from the river, and with blade down picked up brush and anything else that would move. All these crossings required a lot of time and effort.

We finally got everything down the Taylor and into Tok on the Alaska

Highway, where I left with my Cat to go back to Glennallen. I saw the locomotive and a couple of the trailers just south of Fox near Fairbanks years later. I guess they are still there? In my short experience with this massive piece of equipment I came away with great admiration for the men who ran this monster across miles and miles of ice, snow, mountains, and tundra to the Arctic Ocean and back.

Chapter Six
Earthquakes

In 1964, Valdez was hit really hard by an earthquake. A ship was unloading at the Valdez docks when the quake hit, and Donald O'Leary, who was in the truck on the dock when it came, was killed, as was Jimmy Growden. Another driver and his two boys, who were taking a walk on the dock, were also killed. Freddy Brown was another one, and several others. It was a tragic day and a tragic happening. Vic Unfer was also thought to have been drowned or lost on the dock, but was actually up the road toward Copper Center, and he was hung up there for many hours because of the road being broken up and blocked with rocks and stuff from the earthquake. After this earthquake occurred they moved the whole town entirely away from where it was originally situated, back up to more stable ground quite a ways from the original town site.

Chapter Seven
Personal History

My ties to transportation began when I was a young boy. I was raised on a large ranch located on the Ten-Mile River, north of Fort Bragg, California. This ranch was bordered on the west by the Pacific Ocean, and the eastern boundary lay in the hills of the Californian Coast Range, and was heavily timbered with huge redwood trees. Large hayfields were located above the large timber groves on the high ridges. Farming and hauling the hay was accomplished with teams of workhorses. The hay was loaded on wagons, and pulled with four-horse teams. My dad would let me hold the reins and drive the teams when we were on the flat ground. I really looked forward to going with him, and as I grew older I was allowed to drive more and more. When I was about 12 or 13 I was making the whole trip by myself. In 1929, my dad purchased a brand new Model A Ford truck. After a few lessons on how to push the clutch in and so on, I was allowed to drive it—or steer it actually—through the fields as it was being loaded with hay. I remember to this day the thrill of being behind the wheel of that truck.

I also recall a teacher I had in the sixth grade who obviously had very little respect for anyone who drove a truck, and in those days nobody had any respect for them, I believe. Anyway, she would shout at me in class, as I was paying absolutely no attention to her, "Clifford, sit up and pay attention, or you'll grow up to be a truck driver." I can't tell you how many times over the ensuing years I could hear that loud, raspy voice yelling at me as I was worn out and on the tail end of a 30- or 40-hour truck trip. I guess she knew what she was talking about, because I did, in fact, end up as a truck driver most of my life. Two or three days after the new truck arrived on the farm. My father was very proud of it We took it up to a neighbor, Arthur Gray, who owned the neighboring ranch, and after looking and walking around the truck and raising the hood and just generally admiring it, we were all standing around and talking when Arthur Gray looked over in the grass 30 or 40 feet away, and said, "Look over there, there's a damn skunk in that grass." We looked over and sure enough, we could see the black and white back of the skunk. Arthur said to my father, "I've heard that if you hit a skunk in the middle of the back, it will paralyze them and they can't spray their stink. Let's go get a long two-by-four and whack him with it." Arthur went over by the barn and came back with about a 16-foot-long board and both of them crept over close enough to the skunk that with one end planted in the ground, it would strike this intruder square on the back. I recall that pole sticking straight up in the air, and both of them having a firm grasp on it, and agreeing that they had it lined up for a perfect hit on the target. All these preliminary activities were done in almost total silence, when I heard a very quiet, "Now!" and the pole went down straight as an arrow on the target. Everyone stood there for a bit waiting to see if the skunk let loose its nasty-smelling spray. Nothing but clean, pure air prevailed. Arthur said, "We did it. We killed the S.O.B." and it didn't smell. They then walked over to the grass to survey their good deed and lying there, very dead, was this black and white intruder, Arthur's very prized Australian sheepdog. The only thing I heard after a few minutes of silence was Arthur telling my father, "You don't tell anyone about this, and I won't either."

At the start of World War II while waiting for orders to report to boot camp I got a job driving a dump truck in San Francisco at Hunters Point Naval shipyard. The truck was an old Fageol. It was a chain-drive rig with hard rubber tires, a real dinosaur of a truck. After 8 or 10 hours of driving in this contraption you felt like you had been beaten with a chain, but to me it was a great experience, and I knew I wanted to become that truck driver my teacher had predicted I would become. With this first job, I joined the Teamsters Union and have remained a member of the Teamsters all of my lifetime. In World War II, I enlisted in the Army Air Corps, and ended up as a skipper on an air-sea rescue boat. With the end of the war, I returned to Anderson, California. I went to work driving a log truck for the Ralph Smith lumber company, where I stayed for four years driving and did mechanic work in the wintertime. I went to work for Chase Livestock in Redding, hauling cattle for two or three years and eventually purchased my first truck and hauled lumber all up and down the west coast.

My grandfather, Howard Bishop, and two of his friends had gone to the Klondike gold rush in 1898, and brought back many stories of his experiences and also a collection of gold nuggets. I would sit by the hour and listen to the tales of the Far North, such as his going over the Chilkoot Pass and then building a raft and floating down the Yukon River, and through the White Horse rapids, where the raft just in front of them tipped over with three miners on it and two of them drowned. He was able to get a hold of one guy by his collar and pulled him up onto their raft more dead than alive, but they were able to revive him. This man went along with them to the Klondike and worked as a full partner and, in fact, went back to California with my grandfather and worked for him on his ranch until my grandfather passed away. They called him Sparky and I have no clue how he came by that nickname. In fact, the only thing we ever saw with a name on it was an envelope addressed to a Sir Alfred E. Littlewood, which had come from England. This opened up a lot of speculation that perhaps Sparky was from some high-up family in England and was some kind of English lord. This man left soon after Grandfather died, and no one ever heard from him again. We often wondered about his past and if he did indeed return to England.

After they got to Dawson, only to find out, as many others did, that there were no mining claims left to stake out, Howard and the two other would-be miners accompanied by their newfound tagalong hiked back up the river to McQuestion Creek and went to work felling trees and cutting them into boards, to float back downstream to Dawson. Then they sold them to the miners to shore up their claims, since most of the Klondike mining was done by digging down through the tundra, and the walls would be supported and shored up by these boards. This process was called whipsawing. They worked on a bank and rolled the logs out onto a scaffolding, one man on top of the log and one underneath, and using a cross-cut saw, they sawed from one end of the log to the other, resulting in rough-sawn planks. This was backbreaking work, but highly rewarding for each of the men, because one of the men used his earnings to purchase a half interest in one of Dawson's saloons, and the other invested in a rooming house. My grandfather with his newfound friend went back to California and paid off the mortgage on the farm. So from a very early age, I was intrigued by these stories, and loved the lure of the North, and the adventures I felt certain awaited me there.

Chapter Eight
Going North

I pulled into a truck stop in Redding, California one day, after a trip to southern California, and ran into a friend of mine there. We got talking about one of my favorite subjects, going to Alaska. He also had a great interest in that part of the country, because his father had been up there in prior years. I said, "Let's go." He said, "When?" My answer, "Right now." So by golly, we started planning and about three days later we took off from Redding, California and headed north. I was absolutely spellbound by the majestic beauty of the mountains and streams and we were only a couple hundred miles into British Columbia. This whole trip to me was a great awakening, and the farther north I got, the more convinced I was that this was where I wanted to move and make my future. We got into Anchorage, and I inquired around into jobs in trucking, and was told that Mark Moore, one of the true pioneers of Alaska trucking, was looking to hire experienced diesel mechanics. I talked to him, and after learning my background, he said "You can go to work immediately." Well, his side was ready, but mine wasn't. I told him that I was going back to load up my family and head north.

Well, it didn't quite work out that way. After I went back south, it took about another year and a half to get enough money together to make the big move. I got an old International truck and built a pull trailer, which I loaded up with all my earthly belongings, along with my wife and two kids, and we got into Dawson Creek and stayed overnight resting up, doing laundry, and preparing to tackle the formidable Alcan highway, 100 percent unpaved. We had gone about two hours out of Dawson when it started snowing, and the wind blowing, and this continued all of that day and into the next afternoon.

We didn't make very much headway these first couple of days out, but we were still going, and other than rough roads and hitting several other snow squalls, everything was going well. I had been driving many hours, and since it wasn't snowing, I convinced my wife that she should drive for a while and let me rest up. She reluctantly agreed and I fell asleep almost instantly.

An hour or so later I half woke up as the whole rig was kind of jerking along. At first I thought it was rough road, and her foot was bouncing off the throttle but that was not the problem. I immediately came fully awake and told her to stop, got out, walked back to the trailer, and one of the trailer tires was flat, and had worn clear down to the hub, no rubber left on it whatsoever. The whole trailer axle was sticking out the rear end and pointing back toward Dawson Creek. This happened in the vicinity of Kluane Lake, with nothing resembling civilization as far as I could see. Well, after sitting there for an hour or so and no other traffic appearing, I started becoming convinced that we were going to have to abandon the trailer and go for help, when along came a Yukon Road Commission truck with a welder on it, and this gentleman stopped and helped me pull the axle back up into place close to where it belonged, and then with the U-bolts gone, he welded the axle to the spring and we also hooked a chain up to the front of the trailer in case the weld broke, and I was able to salvage enough of the wheel to get the spare tire back on and head up the road to our new life in the north. Everything worked well from that point on.

Chapter Nine
Going to Work in Alaska

We finally arrived in Anchorage, tired and disheveled, thankful to have survived and still grateful to the Yukon road worker who had helped us on our way. The first person I saw was Mark Moore, and he said, "I knew you would come back, but I didn't think it would take you this long." I went to work for him the next morning. Several months later I had the opportunity to go driving for Bob Stratton, the Union Oil dealer in Glennallen, and took the job, for driving was what I had wanted to do in the first place.

This job was driving tanker trucks from Glennallen to Anchorage, two or three days a week, and then spending the rest of the week traveling to the various locations scattered throughout the Interior. Our marketing area was huge, and required hundreds of miles of travel to service all our accounts, for the Union Oil company had the contract for supplying all the heating oil and gas to the schools and the various highway road camps. This marketing area ran from Eureka on the Glenn Highway to Delta Junction, Thompson Pass on the Richardson Highway, and from Glennallen to Tok, and from Tok to Northway on the Alcan, then over the Taylor Highway to Eagle on the Yukon River. I started driving in the summer months, and I started traveling to all the various outlying state road camps and schools, so I learned the roads pretty well before freeze-up.

One of the first trips I made that stands out in my memory was to Eagle on the Yukon River. Eagle was one of the first settlements in the Interior and gained prominence due to its location not too far down the river from Dawson City on the Yukon, where gold was discovered in 1898. To get to Eagle required a trip of some 160 miles off the Alcan

Highway over a road called the Taylor Highway. This journey starts at Tetlin on the Alaska Highway, 11 miles south of Tok, and takes you through some majestic country, an old mining town called Chicken, and through the historic Forty-Mile mining district. You connect with what is called the Top of the World Highway at 96 miles in from Tetlin; at Jack Wade Junction the road continues 79 miles to Dawson City, Yukon Territory, and makes a left turn at this point. You are on your way to Eagle, another 69 miles that back in the early days was a road that challenged your driving skills. If you allowed your thoughts to wander, you might think that this so-called highway resembled a road. Wrong. It actually was closer to being at best a trail through the Alaska wilderness. I recall prior to my very first trip to Eagle, I asked an old-timer by the name of Jack Wallace, "How long does it take to drive into Eagle?" Jack thought for a moment before he responded. "Cliff," he said, "take off your wristwatch and take a calendar." He was absolutely right. The road was a real challenge and on the 12 or 15 trips I made on it I felt it was a good time if I could do it in 10 or 12 hours—and that was only one way. The hills were long and steep, the road was narrow and if it rained you could plan on putting chains on, since the roadbed would turn into a gooey mess and traction became nearly impossible. And of course, any time after mid-September you could bet there would be snow on the higher passes.

The road being totally closed for about five months of the year, we had to go in as late as possible to top off the tanks, all the heating oil tanks for the road commission and the schools, and then get back as soon as we could after breakup in the spring, since by then the tanks were always getting close to empty. These late fall and early spring trips always proved to be very challenging. We had to cross many places where the ice had glaciered across the road, totally across the road, making these spots extremely dangerous. As in all cases, the ice was thicker toward the inside of the road, and tapered toward the outside, and in most places from the outside edge it was a very steep drop, sometimes as much as a thousand feet to the bottom—a situation that commanded your total and undivided attention. I got into a huge rainstorm in midsummer on one trip and of course I had to chain up. It was very slow going, but all was going well until I got into a sharp right-hand turn, and all of a sudden my rear axle on the trailer got over into some really heavy muck. Although I had my tractor well up on the upside of the road, the trailer slid off until the right rear duals were hanging over the edge in midair. It was 40 or 50 feet straight down there and I was totally across the road with no way of getting out. I sat there for two or three hours, and finally a pickup truck came along who was also headed into Eagle. I got him to go back to Forty-Mile Roadhouse, 35 or 40 miles back down the road, to where they had radio contact with the Tok road camp, 60 or 70 miles away. I had them call back to Glennallen and dispatch another one of our trucks up there in order to pump my load off to enable us to get my rig back on its feet. The road commission had a small Caterpillar 15 or so miles up the road, which they walked back to my rig, and once we got most of the load pumped off, we were able to pull it out. Although there were only five or six cars going either way in or out of Eagle, they got totally shut down for about 30 hours, and I don't think they were very happy with me, for they named this particular spot Union Oil Corner, and it lived in infamy from then on, I guess.

None of the trips were ever dull. I always tried to take off from the Forty-Mile Roadhouse on the Alaska Highway, where the Taylor Highway began. Always tried to leave very early in the morning and would go in and unload as much as I could that day. I would finish up the second day and start the return trip. I always looked forward to this run, because you could depend on seeing wildlife; at times there were very big herds of caribou and I usually saw moose and bears. I used to take a lot of caribou meat out of this area, and the occasional moose. I had never killed a grizzly bear so I decided to carry my rifle on some of these trips and sure enough, I ran across a very large grizzly. He walked across right in front of me and about 60, 70 yards away. It was a golden grizzly, who didn't seem to be bothered at all by the fact that my truck was rolling toward him. I slowed down and got to a total stop. I probably wasn't 50 yards from him when I stopped. He was just crawling up the bank and I immediately set my tractor parking brakes. The bear was slowly walking up the bank beside the road and was paying absolutely no attention to me. I grabbed my gun and got out and was taking aim on the bear when I noticed that my truck was moving. The brakes that were on my tractor, the parking brakes, weren't holding it, since I was on a downhill slope, so I jumped back up in the cab, reached over and pulled the trailer brake handle on. This, of course, stopped the truck immediately. I quickly twisted around and jumped back out with my rifle. In so doing I engaged the cord from the air horn that was attached down toward the dash, and with that loud blast of the air horn, by the time my feet hit the ground that bear was at full speed disappearing into the brush. I decided that using a truck for bear hunting was not a great idea.

Chapter Ten
Winter Operations and Experiences

With this early- and late-summer Alaska driving, we were ready to face our first round of Alaska winter. With this job I had started my Alaska driving career, which kept me driving for others or owning my own equipment over the next 40-plus years. We really liked Glennallen, and after a few months, we knew that this would be our home for a long time to come. Just before winter set in, we purchased a mobile home and moved it to where the fuel storage tanks were located. There was no running water, so we purchased a 300-gallon tank, built a heated water storage shed, and hauled water to it in order to have showers and wash dishes and for general purposes. We used honey buckets for our toilet needs. With this done, we thought we were ready for winter. We had a lot to learn about that.

We had a rude awakening about the time the first cold weather hit. With no insulated skirting on the base of the mobile home, the floor got very cold and by December if you spilled water on the floor, it turned to instant ice. I knew right away that this setup was no way to face an Alaska winter. We managed to survive with no ill effects. The first thing after spring breakup I got a backhoe and dug a septic tank and put a whole lot of insulation under the bottom of the trailer. My old Kenworth I drove that first winter was relegated to the cold with no inside storage. Although I had an engine heater that could be plugged into an electric outlet, it was only good to about 30 below zero, and if the temperature started to drop below that, I started the engine and let it run until leaving on my next trip.

I recall one very cold night I came in late and connected the engine heater to the electric outlet, went inside and right to bed. In the morning when I went out to start my truck it was unplugged, and it took almost two hours to get it cranked up. I was dumbfounded that it wasn't plugged in, because I was certain I had done this before going inside. Well, the next evening when I got in I again plugged in the heater and went inside. About an hour later, upon looking out the window I observed my German shepherd puppy tugging at the electric cord and immediately solved the mystery. I didn't kill the dog but I did secure the electric cord so the pup didn't do it again.

If a real cold spell hit I sometimes let the truck run a week or more at a time, turning it off only long enough to check the oil. Even though I had done a lot of winter driving in the snow prior to moving to Alaska, having to haul through the Sierra Nevada and eastern Oregon, nothing had prepared me for the extreme temperatures of Alaska. Having hit temperatures that first winter lower than minus 70, it was quite an experience, to say the least, learning how to dress for these temperatures—the types of shoes, the Arctic gear. I found that the very best gear were the army surplus boots, which had the air valves built in, and snowmachine suits were also very functional. Topping off everything was an arctic parka, with wolverine fur on the facepiece—because the fur does not freeze. With all of the above pieces of clothing—along with mittens with liners inside— I have delivered heating oil in temperatures of 70 below and have managed to stay at it for six or seven hours at a time. Though not pleasant, with the correct clothing it was possible to function in these extreme temperatures.

The equipment was another story. There was no dressing it up to contend with the cold. I had an awful lot of things to learn about the cold and how to cope with running in these extreme temperatures. I found out real soon that if you didn't have inside storage for your truck when parked, your problems increased to a large degree. At times you would park the rig with temperatures in the minus 20s and 30s and wake in the a.m. at 40 below or worse, and this made it a necessity to preheat your oil pan or risk knocking a bearing out upon starting. The tool of choice was a weed burner, and I soon found out that it was an absolute necessity for winter survival in the extreme temperatures of the Interior back in the old days before they came out with Arctic-grade diesel oil and greases that are available nowadays. The weed burner consisted of a simple 5-gallon propane bottle with a 2-foot piece of pipe with a burner head attached and a rubber hose with a fitting attached to the bottle. The propane was always carried on the outside of the truck to ensure that the driver would not be exposed to a possible gas leak. If the hose was left attached to the bottle you had to be very careful not to straighten it out before heating it up, because it would break like glass.

This little beauty could be used for many things. For example, placed directly onto the exposed diesel fuel tank we could heat up the fuel to keep it from becoming a solid mass of Jello, like goo that would in no way flow through the lines of the fuel pump. It could also be used to heat the cab of a cold truck by turning it to a low setting and being careful not to ignite anything inside; it would soon be nice and warm. This was very handy in starting a rig that had been shut down for a period of time, heating the oil up in the pan and getting operational again. We used pieces of stovepipe with an elbow attached to one end, laid the pipe on the ground with the elbow pointing up toward the pan, and put the burner into the other end, and in a short while you had a pan full of nice warm oil that assured you of oil pressure when starting the engine. I've seen it so cold that when lighting the burner, the resultant flame was not more than a 3- or 4-inch flickering flame. To cure this, we put the flame directly onto the propane bottle and soon had a hot burning torch to work with. It could also be used to firepot transmissions and rear ends if needed—all in all a very handy and much used tool in the Far North.

Prior to the propane-fired torches we used the old kerosene burners, which didn't work very well at extreme temperatures. You had to carry along a can of white gas and a gas torch to preheat the kerosene in order to get it to generate and give off a good flame, so it was a real blessing to use the propane outfit instead. I always mounted a thermometer on the outside rear view mirror brackets, for they recorded temperatures to 80 below. I was going into Tok on my first trip with the temperature below minus 70. The temperature in Glennallen was 58 below zero and when I got to the Mentasta Pass it got to 67 or 68 below. By the time I got into Tok, it was under 70 below. The last few miles before Tok, the road was straight as an arrow, and when I got to the Parker House service station, located on the right side, I turned my wheel and it was like it had been welded. I turned it as hard as I could, and got it to just barely move. These rigs at the time did not have power steering. The end result was that I had to heat up the steering box with my trusty torch and mix some diesel with the grease in the steering sector box order to get it to turn. I eventually got it into Anchorage and into Mark Moore's shop and replaced the grease with a lightweight oil.

I had many things happen that first winter that let me know that this Alaska living was something that had best be taken seriously or you could end up in dire straits. When you are driving down the road in a warm car or truck, and you happen to have a mechanical problem, and the truck or the engine or your vehicle is shut down for mechanical reasons, in temperatures of 40 or more below, it suddenly becomes a matter of survival. People don't understand how cold that is. Basically, your deep freeze at home runs from about zero to about 10 above zero, and is called a deep freeze, so at 40, 50, 60, or 70 below you're in deep trouble if you are stuck out there very long. Not only is it possible for these things to happen, they do happen.

One night when coming out of Anchorage, I was about 10 miles out of Glennallen, and it was very cold, approximately minus 58 degrees. I came upon a station wagon parked on the road with no lights on, so I pulled up alongside, took my flashlight, slid over on the passenger side of my truck, and looked down into the car. There was nobody inside, so I took off. About a half mile down the road, I saw something in my headlights. As I got closer, I saw it was a person, staggering up the road. I stopped and got down from the cab and saw this woman nearly frozen. I managed to get her up into the truck. She was very lightly dressed in only a sweater and slacks. I asked her what happened with her car. She said it was running fine and then it just quit. I told her that I had stopped and looked into it and not seen anyone there, and had driven along down the road. She said, "Oh, my God, my kids were in the car." I said, "I bet they got out of the car after you left, because there was nobody in the car." I put the truck in reverse with my backup lights on and backed all the way to the car. I jumped out with flashlight in hand and found both of the kids cuddled up under an old blanket behind the front seat. I got the kids up into the truck took them on into Glennallen. I got a hold of Terry Fisher to go back with me and tow the car back to his shop. It took us at least another hour and a half, and in that time not another single car came by in either direction, so it could have ended up a complete disaster. The kids were like icicles when I got them out of the car. I can't say for certain that no other vehicle would have come by after that, but it is certainly possible that it would have been long enough that the outcome would have been much different had I not come along when I did.

Over the years of driving—and I'm sure that most drivers have had the same thing occur—you are going to run across many and varied situations where people have shut down for mechanical reasons, and low temperatures usually seem to bring out the bad traits of a car or truck We stop many times and assist these people and most of them are not prepared. If they had to stay there very long, they would not survive it. But most people don't realize the seriousness of traveling through this type of temperature. On another occasion two fellows were headed to Tok on the Tok Cutoff when their car broke down approximately 8 miles out of town. So, after waiting for several hours in temperatures near 60 below, they decided to walk and by the time someone came along both had frozen feet that required amputation of their toes, and at that they were very fortunate. They had walked only 3 miles. It was very lucky for them to have escaped with their lives.

I had finished servicing my accounts in Tok, and it was extremely cold, down in the deep 50s below zero. I was leaving there about ten o'clock at night and was headed back toward Glennallen. I saw a car on the road in his lane, headed toward Tok, and I couldn't make it out at first because his headlights were really dim. They were barely emitting any light. I pulled up alongside the vehicle to look down into the car, and observed a man with his head lying on the steering wheel. I rolled down my window and hollered at him. He didn't flinch, so I blew my air horn and he came up off the steering wheel like he'd been shot and looked around and finally glanced over and saw my truck. I motioned to him to roll his window down, and told him to step on the throttle and speed the engine up. As he did this, his headlights immediately came back up bright. What had happened is that he had run out of eyeballs and had stopped to rest with his car idling. It was an older model car that had a generator instead of an alternator, and it had quit charging as opposed to a car equipped with an alternator, which will charge even at idle speed. I told him to shut off his headlights and keep his engine running at that fast idle until he charged his battery. I sat there for about 10 minutes, then told him to let the car idle and turn the headlights back on. He did so, and his lights were good and bright. He was a soldier transferring from Alaska to the South 48 and was accompanied by his wife and two children. I told him to get on the road and not to stop until he got to Tok. I told him that if he stopped again and the car quit that he could possibly expose his whole family to freezing to death as I was probably the last one on the road for the rest of the night. I can assure you, he was wide awake by this time. I sat there for another two or three minutes and watched the taillights disappear down the road. They were very fortunate, since the car was within minutes of completely shutting down. Going down on the road toward Glennallen for another two or three hours, I didn't see another car. I often wonder what the outcome of that situation would have been had I not happened along when I did. They were fortunate to have escaped with their existence.

After the first two or three years we learned a lot about the Alaska winters; however, looking back on it, we had gotten only a brief glimpse of what was to come over the next 40 years or more, when a Chinook wind could leave a road with water running on pure ice. I have had my truck and trailer slide sideways while sitting dead still, fully loaded The whole truck would slide sideways off the road with no forward momentum whatsoever, just by the fact that it was so slick and there was enough of a slope on the road toward the ditch that the truck slid in that direction. We carried a set of chains that we called doubled-up singles. You'd take a set of single chains and put an extra set of crossbars in them, and double the number of crossbars, giving much better traction. Under these conditions we'd throw one of these chains over on the driver's-side steering axle to keep the front end of the truck from sliding toward the ditch, and along with the drive axles, chained up with chains that are called three-railers, which covered the dual tires on the drivers. Sometimes we'd even use two chains on the front end, if the road conditions were bad enough; in most cases, however, one chain was ample. We also put chains on the left rear trailer tires to keep the trailer from sliding off as well. With all these chains on, your truck had a great tendency to keep going straight down the road and out of the ditch. You would be better off just to park the miserable things until conditions improved; in most cases, however, you were in a hurry and didn't want to wait, and so you chained up and kept going. And that's how we did it.

One of the things we have to contend with in low temperatures is the wheels locking up when you stop, even for a short period of time. This happens when you apply your brakes to stop, thereby creating enough heat to melt a bit of the ice accumulated in and around the brake drums, which runs to the bottom of the wheel and in low temperatures, in very short order, freezes back down, making it impossible for the wheel to turn. If this happens and the driver goes on down the road with one or more wheels locked up, it's a very short period of time before the tires wear clear through, leaving nothing but useless pieces of rubber and a very embarrassed driver. You would have to remove the ruined tires and replace them with a spare, or single out one of the other axles to get on down the road. It is a very difficult task in the dark and cold. This tire situation was combated by painting stripes on all the trailer wheels that were mounted to the outside; on starting up we did a series of S turns in the first few hundred feet, and watched out the rearview mirror to make certain that each wheel was turning by watching the painted stripes turn. The same procedure was used at night by switching on the powerful backup lights that are directed toward the trailer tires. If, in fact, a wheel was locked up, we always carried a 3- or 4-pound hammer, and by hitting the brake drum a sharp blow, it would break up the ice and release. You would think that with a loaded truck it would be easy to feel one or more wheels not turning, but on ice-covered roads you drive along very nicely until ruined. And again, it always amazed me how fast this could happen; even running on the ice, the friction created there actually does not take too long to wear them down and they are gone. After this has happened to you one or more times, you are aware of not slamming the brakes on really fast if possible. You also don't set your parking brakes unless you are on a hill and there are no other options. In later years they used a plastic piece about an inch wide; it hooks on to one of the lug bolts on the outside duals and protrudes out a few inches beyond the tire. You see it turning around and it really is better than the stripes because it is easier to see. In spite of all the precautions a driver can take, these things still occur, because at times when it's snowing or the wind is blowing, and the snow swirling around, it is impossible to see 10 feet out of your rearview mirror, so you take off anyway and hope everything is okay.

In wintertime in Copper Center, a young lady and her husband living there had a baby. I believe the baby was about three or four months old, and it unfortunately passed away from SIDS, Sudden Infant Death Syndrome. The end result, normally speaking, is that you are going to have to wait until spring to do a burial because of the ground being frozen. This young lady came to me and pleaded with me to try and get a grave dug, since I owned a backhoe at the time. I told her it was impossible. I finally agreed to go and try to dig a grave. The spot was just out there in the Glennallen area, so I went out and worked all one day. I raised the backhoe up in the air as high as it would go, and let it go, chipping out little pieces at a time. I finally got a spot dug probably about 16 or 18 inches deep. I was ready to give up on the thing, and then Jim Johnson, a very dear friend of mine, suggested that I dig out a little deeper, if I could, big enough to get the little casket into it; then we would put what dirt we had over it and get it covered back up. He would bring a dump truck in the spring and haul a load of dirt in to make a decent grave out of it. So that was what we did, but it was one of the hardest jobs and such a disaster for the young couple. A really hard job. I was glad I was able to do it for them.

We were up in Tok in January, and several of us had stayed overnight at the Parker House Motel. The temperatures were approximately 35 below when we shut down. I left my truck running, for I didn't want to get up early in the morning and start out delivering heating oil in a cold rig. And upon awakening, I was glad I had—the temperatures were pushing minus 60 degrees. After making three or four deliveries in the area I came back to the Parker House for some breakfast, hot coffee, and to warm up. After I sat there for a few minutes, one of the fellows came into the restaurant and said, "Boy, did I ever screw up by not letting my truck run last night," and asked if I had a weed burner he could borrow. I said, "Sure," and told him to go ahead and take it off the rig and use it because I was waiting for my breakfast order. He came back inside about the time I finished breakfast and said, "I got her started up," and ordered a cup of coffee, and about three or four minutes later this kid in the service station ran in and said, "Your truck is on fire!" We both jumped up and ran out and sure enough, a big bunch of smoke was swirling in and around the cab; however, the motor was running along just fine. He yanked the door open and jumped up to shut the engine off and with the door open, the smoke soon disappeared. His truck was equipped with a main and auxiliary transmission, as were all the big rigs in those days. We always put the main transmission into a lower gear when left running and with the auxiliary in neutral, the gears would keep turning in the main box and also would keep the driveline turning in the auxiliary box, thereby keeping these units from freezing up the gear oil. In cold starting, such as he had done, and the truck having sat there for many hours at 55 or 60 below zero, the gear oil gets like tar and what had happened was that in putting his truck into a low gear, setting the throttle at 1,000 rpm, and letting the clutch out, everything was turning except the transmission. The clutch was slipping and in a very few minutes was completely burned out. He had not put any heat on his transmission and paid the price. I've seen the same exact thing on cold-starting an engine, and after running for a couple of minutes—a big clunk, and the end result was a locked-up bearing and an expensive overhaul.

The winters in Alaska can cost you dearly if you ignore the deep cold but on the other hand, operating in temperatures in the mid to low minus 70s is very possible if done correctly. I have delivered heating oil in Tok and Northway in temperatures exceeding 76 below zero. Although I have done this, I don't believe there is any way for me or anyone else to describe in written words what these temperatures feel like to someone who has not experienced them firsthand. And if you're working outside, even with a face mask and wearing an arctic parka, your lungs will start feeling the effects if you overexert yourself and start deep breathing. That really becomes a test of your endurance.

I recall a situation when I was running across the Palmer flats toward Glennallen, followed by another truck driven by Marvin Glaze. The wind was blowing very hard, 50 to 55 miles per hour, and with the temperatures around plus 40 degrees it is known as a Chinook. The Chinook occurs in a matter of hours, going from freezing temperatures to water standing on top of pure ice. With the wind blowing as it did, along with the ice, my rig began an uncontrolled slide to the left side of the road, across the oncoming lane of traffic and to the very edge of the road, where I hit some gravel. This stopped my slide and sent me back across to the proper lane. Fortunately, there was no traffic coming toward me. I looked into my mirror and watched the other truck do the exact same thing with the same end result. It was a hairy situation, considering that we were both loaded with gasoline, which could have ended up causing a disaster. We managed to get stopped and put a full complement of chains on and continued up toward King Mountain at a slow rate of speed. We came to a little hill across King River where a couple of cars were in the ditch and a semi had spun out. We had to stop. I had to walk gingerly to keep from falling down. With a little tow of this one truck I felt I could pull him back on the road and get him started up the hill again to clear the road. The cars were out of the way, they were all actually in the ditch. I hollered to Marvin right behind me to bring me a chain, so he started dragging the chain up the road just strung out behind him. He wasn't carrying it, he was dragging it. Another truck came up behind us going a little bit fast. Marvin saw that he couldn't get out of the way and the truck couldn't stop because it had slid sideways and started to jackknife, but it did finally manage to stop. I went back and the driver said, "My God, I just ran over a guy in the road." I looked around and then looked underneath the trailer and I still didn't see him. Twenty-five or 30 feet off the snow berm I heard Marvin. He came crawling up and I said, "What the hell happened? How did you get over there?" And he said, "Well, just before the truck hit me I jumped straight up in the air. It batted me like a baseball, and I flew right through the air and over into the ditch." I guess it saved him, but it was a very close scrape for Marvin.

One of the hazards of driving on the Alaska roads is you get what is called ice fog, which falls from the sky in subzero temperatures. It comes out so freezing cold that it is real powdery and light and not all that deep, and doesn't impair your forward motion or anything, but when you get another car or truck, especially a truck, that throws a cloud up in front of your face, that will absolutely totally make you lose all forward vision. It can become quite precarious, because you will never know whether a vehicle is stopped right ahead of you or what the case may be. It certainly gives you a few moments of being totally alert and not being able to avoid it. The only thing you see is one coming toward you leaving a large cloud of swirling snow to drive into, and you slow down before you get up alongside it because you can't anticipate what's going to happen once you meet that vehicle. The better drivers will slow down when they see you coming, but a lot of them won't. It's quite an experience, especially on narrow, two-lane roads. For a few moments it sort of makes you hold your breath and hope nothing is there that you will slam into. People tend to forget in Alaska how extremely serious this cold weather can be.

There is a road that runs from Paxson to Cantwell and Mt. McKinley; the original road into Mt. McKinley, 135 miles long. It was completed in 1957. With the building of the Parks Highway, which was opened in 1971, you can get to McKinley by the Parks Highway now, but in years past they used to have to go up the Richardson Highway, turn off at Paxson, and go across this backwoods gravel road to get to the park. This road is not maintained in the winter months. A family consisting of a grandfather, grandmother, and grandson drove up this road a short ways and the car got hung up. They weren't that far from civilization actually, but in a very short time they were all dead. They couldn't get out of there, and froze to death right there in the car. It is a serious situation, and I've seen so many cases where this could have occurred and didn't. But for the sheer fortune of somebody coming along or somebody interceding, more people would have died.

In running Alaska, over the years you learn to carry a lot of tools, hand tools, a good tool box, always a supply of extra belts. Another thing that is very important is antifreeze. I always carried at least one case of it, because out in that frozen waste there isn't any water anywhere. You break a radiator hose, you can usually repair the hose, but where do you get the water? You just about have to carry antifreeze if you don't want to sit for hours because of lack of water. The other thing in running a truck for any period of time—I always carried an extra alternator along. Alternator problems could shut you down at a moment's notice. Your juice didn't last long in those freezing temperatures. Another item was the repair kits for the air hoses and air lines. You'd continually get ice building up on them, building up and building up, and then get to the point that it actually broke the lines. They were cold, and getting hit by a chunk of ice would break them. So you were always having air line problems, and it was very important to take along the extra hoses, extra ferrules, and fittings. I always carried a supply of them, and it got me out of many a fix over the years. Fuel filters were also an absolute must, especially in the old days when they used what we called number 2 diesel, because it got gummed up and there was no choice but to change your filter out, especially the old sock filters which had the insert sock in them. They were horrible on getting gummed up so I always carried extra fuel filters. It was a case of carrying an extra or having to wait for someone to come along who did have one.

As with most everything that the cold weather in the North handed you, countermeasures were thought up. They came up with a system that circulated water from the radiator through the fuel tanks, thereby keeping the fuel from jelling. It worked very well. They finally came out with what is called -60 degree diesel.

One other item that was an absolute must and certainly doesn't come at the end of the list was jumper cables, battery jumper cables. Forevermore, a truck that sat for any period of time would require an assist to get started, especially in cold weather. You'd be amazed how fast the batteries would run down and how little it took if they didn't kick off right away. I remember we used to pull the compression release on the old-time rigs and roll them over and try to get an indication of oil pressure before we released the compression release to make certain that we were getting oil to the bearings. Sometimes it took a long while for this to occur, creating a large drain on the batteries.

I came in off the road on a cold night, and I had acquired a new little German shepherd puppy. It was 35 to 40 below zero when I got in and I got to the house and found out that she was missing. I looked all over for her. I finally figured that someone had picked her up along the Glenn Highway, and had simply hauled her off. I decided to take one last look outside and my other dog came running up to a little two-wheeled camper trailer, which had snow and ice almost halfway up on the wheels. The big dog got down on its front legs and was looking underneath and wagging its tail. It was impossible for me to get underneath, but I looked underneath with a flashlight and there was this little puppy, with her tongue stuck to the trailer axle. Apparently she had tried to lick the axle when her tongue instantly stuck to it. It was impossible to crawl under there because all the ice and snow had built up around it, completely encasing it in ice, so I took some hot water and poured it on the axle. There was kind of an angle on the axle and I poured it from the uphill side. It ran down the axle, and after about three or four cans of warm water it reached down the spot where her tongue was and she finally came loose. The end result of this was that the puppy's tongue stuck out of her mouth several inches, and after about a week or so, the tongue had sloughed off and approximately one third of it actually disappeared. Finally, after a couple of weeks, I had to hand-feed the puppy. I put sloppy food into the coffee can and just kind of shoved her mouth down into it, and then she just inhaled it. She learned to eat that way—she put her mouth down in it and as long as it was kind of milky or not heavy food she would just suck it up and got very good at it. She survived, and I finally gave her to a friend of mine, who said that she had a litter of puppies later on down the road and the only problem she had was that they had to help clean them off. She couldn't do it with her tongue like that; it really affected her ability to clean the puppies up. She lived to a ripe old age.

A bunch of young kids were having a weekend at Eureka Lodge; they would take snowmachines and tie a rope onto a big truck tube. The kids got onto the tube and the snowmachine would go scooting across the snow, pulling the kids along. It was a lot of fun. Except one day a kid was running the snow-machine, with a little girl in the tube behind him, and he made a sharp turn and consequently the two went flying off like a whiplash. The sled went in underneath his pickup truck, hit the girl and she hit her head on the bottom of the pickup truck. It killed her. So these fun things can sometimes turn into deadly tragedies.

Chapter Eleven
Equipment Then and Now

A never-ending problem back in the early days was our air systems freezing up in the winter months. The air compressors create a large amount of moisture. This goes through the whole system and has a nasty habit of freezing air valves, and at times the main lines that run to the main storage tanks freeze. The trailer seems to cause most problems by freezing the triple valve and either locking up the brakes or making it altogether inoperable. A quick cure for this is alcohol poured directly into the air lines after they are temporarily disconnected from the trailer. This method is only an emergency fix, for they now have air dryers mounted directly in the air tanks and they work very well. The old system used an alcohol bottle mounted in the system that allowed alcohol to feed into the valves and assist them when the brakes were applied. I'd been having many valve freeze-ups, so I stopped by Mark Moore's shop in Anchorage and had one of his alcohol units installed on the truck. The next night I was on the Tok Cutoff road and temperatures were in the minus-40 range. In spite of my new alcohol unit, my air system ran down low enough that the trailer brakes were close to locking up because of the low air pressure, so I stopped and started taking lines apart, and not finding any problems, I took the main line off the alcohol bottle and could see something inside. I got my flashlight and sure enough I could see ice in it. I turned my head to grab a screwdriver to poke it out when a plug of ice about 2 inches long shot out and grazed my left temple, just missing my eye. I believe that would have killed me if it had hit squarely, since it had approximately 120 pounds of air pressure behind it when it shot out. After that initial hang-up the system worked very well. In later years they came up with the air-drying system which solved most of the moisture problems. This is called a spitter, because every few minutes it spits out a charge of air and moisture.

The steering on the early-day trucks could be a real problem in subzero temperatures. It was certainly a great assist when they started putting power steering units on. It just made a world of difference. Not so much when you were driving down the roads at higher speeds, but maneuvering around the yard and backing up and so forth it made a huge difference. You just broke your back on some of those old trucks to get them to turn the wheel in about 30 or 40 below zero back in the days before they came up with arctic-grade lubricants. After sitting in subzero temperatures, rear ends often got so cold as to necessitate firepotting them before taking off, because they'd be so stiff that in many cases the drive line broke upon trying to move the rig. This was especially true of the old-style worm-drive-gear rear ends. There have been great advances in this field with the introduction of the ring-and-pinion-style rear ends equipped with air lockers. This allows the driver to flip an air valve and it engages both rear ends to lock up and drive in tandem, greatly increasing traction, a great help in the conditions in which we operate here in Alaska.

The suspension systems that are used today are a great improvement over the old-style heavy-duty leaf springs. Also, in most cases there was a rubber-mount-type Hendrikson suspension system and also a torsion bar. They call it a torsion bar system. A large steel rod was used one on each side of the drive wheels and each bar was marked with an R or an L, designating right or left. These bars were stressed to operate only in the correct position, and if placed on the wrong side, would break the moment the load was placed on them. I know this is a fact, for I recall going out in the middle of the night on the Richardson Highway near Thompson Pass and working three or four hours installing one on a loaded truck that had broken down. Upon letting the jacks off and putting the load back on, it popped like a cannon, and broke apart. My boss had loaded this bar up in the dark and obviously got the wrong one. Needless to say, by the time we got back to the shop and got another one and installed it, the night was gone and also part of the morning. Many different suspensions were used, most of them based on leaf springs and many of them worked very well. However, these systems were very rough riding on both the driver and the loads. They took a beating. Today's system uses what is called the air ride. It uses a series of air bags both on the trucks and trailers, and just made a whole lot of difference in the quality of the ride and the comfort you get using this system. It also protects the cargo and saves many dollars on freight damage, which occurred on the old systems.

One of the biggest improvements in equipment was the replacement of the old rayon tires which were referred to as rag tires, with the new nylon tires. The old rayon tires would flatten out after sitting for a short while and depending on the temperature at the time, would shake your eyeteeth out until they rounded out again. One of the biggest advantages was the improved traction. Another great plus was if you got a flat tire with the nylon you could run for a long ways compared to the rayon, because the rayon would self-destruct if run very far while flat, because of the valve stem whipping around inside the tire. There was a lot of experimenting with tires in the Far North trying to get better traction. They tried using coil wires imbedded inside the rubber recaps, which, when run for a short while, would wear enough to expose these wire ends to the road, supposedly to improve traction. They called this type of tire a wobbly wire. I tried them a couple of times but couldn't tell much difference. They also tried using cork imbedded in the rubber. Again, this was a lost cause since it didn't help traction that much and wore out twice as fast as regular recaps. We also tried using studded tires, and in the end with the nylon tire being put into service, we gave up on all these other experiments.

Transmissions have progressed over the years from the old single transmission, used for many years with deep reduction gears at lower speeds, to four- or five-speed main transmissions, to include an auxiliary transmission mounted behind the main with three- or four-speed capability, making a variety of combinations of gears available at all speeds and road conditions. Plus, many trucks were equipped with an additional two-speed rear differential, which could be activated by flipping a switch on the shift stick or on the dash to a high or low range as needed. Some of the old trucks I have driven were equipped with an additional shift stick to shift the rear end with. This made a total of three gear shifts to contend with and this combined with the fact that the horsepower in those days was usually somewhere around 150, meant that you stayed real busy selecting gears. Transmissions since the old days have turned back around to single units, with the 10-, 13- and 18-speed transmissions being the most popular. These units are equipped with a selector located on the top end of the gear shift and with a flip of a finger you can select high or low in any gear while in the high range. Another selector is used for shifting from low to high range; the range selector is always low to start with, and after going through about half of the available gears, it is switched into high range. The same exact gear pattern that we used in low range now becomes your higher speed used for highway travel. So from two or three shift levers to one, with gear selection done by fingerpower, this is a vast improvement. Back when the two transmission combinations were used, the shifting of these gears was considered an art form by the drivers and they got to be very adept at handling these sticks.

I remember one story I heard about two old-time drivers, Jack Steele, and another one called Scarface Scotty. Jack hitched a ride with Scotty on a dark winter night and as they were starting up the winding steep hills on the Glenn Highway, Scotty reached up and switched the overhead cab light on and started grabbing gears. In a short while he looked over at Jack and said, "Pretty good, huh?" Jack said, "I do it the same, exact way, only better." Each driver had a lot of pride in how well he could shift these transmissions. There was also a vast difference in these old transmissions, since in the 7,000 series boxes, they had what we referred to as square gears, which were very difficult to shift. You had only a split second to get these gears to mesh, for the engine speed had to be just right to coincide with the drive line speed, and if not synchronized, the end result was the grinding of gears, and your hand and wrist felt like they had been hit by a hammer. With the old transmissions, it was a great help to make use of the so-called clutch brake. When the clutch pedal was completely depressed, if you shoved a little harder this would en- gage the clutch brake located on the input shaft of the transmission, and this in turn slowed up the gears, allowing you to shift. It was a great assist, if you knew how to use it. With these new transmissions, most drivers use the clutch only when first putting the truck in gear and from then on, any and all gear changes are accomplished without ever touching the clutch again. When you had mastered the mysteries of all these various gears, which some never did, you were able to make good progress over the road. It was not uncommon in those days to see a truck stopped dead still while on the way up a steep hill, having missed a gear, not being able to pick up lower ones. The end result was you stopped and started off in the lowest gear you had, and in most cases stayed there until you reached the top of the hill.

The 7,000 series boxes were replaced by the 8,000 series and this was a vast improvement. The so-called square gears were replaced by synchronized gears, making them much easier to shift. Among the things that went along with this two-stick mode of shifting were stick extensions, which were usu- ally available in lengths of 6 to 8 inches or more and were shaped in various angles, usually 15 to 30 degrees. These extensions were attached to the top end of the shift levers and were highly chromed, and were also available for many different sizes, shapes, and colors of shift knobs to be put on the end of these extensions. The result was that some of these combinations were a sight to behold, but each was put together by the individual driver, supposedly to make his shifting abilities better. I recall seeing a truck turned over near

Modesto, California many years ago. It had been hauling a load of tomatoes and they were scattered all over the place, a real mess. The road was closed and over the next hour or so, being curious, some of us wandered down by the overturned truck, and looked in the cab. It was a sight I'll never forget. The shift stick was protruding up into the steering wheel. The truck was in a left-hand turn and he shifted with the steering wheel turned to the left and as a result the wheel could not be straightened out, since the shift stick was sticking through it, and over the bank he went.

Another transmission that is being used in big rigs is the automatic. I personally never liked this, probably because my experiences with it were all bad. The first truck I had with an automatic transmission caught fire and burned. That truck had a built-in so-called retarder, that when engaged gave a braking action going downhill. My driver was on his way to Los Angeles and dropping down off the grapevine when with the retarder engaged, back pressure built up and the fluid squirted onto the exhaust, through the filler tube. The end result was a burned-up truck. I leased a rig in Alaska one winter when one of my trucks was in for repairs and it was equipped with an automatic transmission. The thing I didn't care for was that in dropping off a hill—and this is in the winter time—it would downshift automatically and it was a rather severe change. On several occasions my wheels had a tendency to lock up, thereby causing a sliding motion, which is not a very good feeling. Applying the throttle then corrected it, but I didn't like it because of that reason. I think they're fine on flat country but not on ice. It did not work very well for me.

In the diesel truck the engine has evolved over the years from a very low horsepower to today's monster engines, developing up to more than 600 horsepower and more. This transformation took place over many years of trial and error, and that included all today's engines, Caterpillar, Cummins, and GMC being the most widely used. Over many years these engines of today carry long-lasting warranties, up to three years and 500,000 miles, so it is very obvious that these engines are all extremely well built and reliable. I personally had more experience in the early days with the Cummins engine, but have since owned and driven many Cats and GMCs, and did not have any great preference for one over the other. In the early days of the Cummins, I started out driving their old 150-horsepower engines. They then came out with a 200-horsepower edition. After the 200 showed up, I recall them using the sleeves out of the 200 and putting them into the old 150 block, making it a 165-horsepower rig. Then they added a 200-horsepower model and Roots blower plus other modifications, making a 275-horsepower and then a 300-horsepower version. And these engines, over the years, with different adaptations such as exhaust-driven turbo, created many different horsepower ranges from 150 to 165 to 200 to 220, 250, 262, 275, 300 and up, and somewhere in between there were others available. I do recall that the early Cummins engines were equipped with a cone-shaped device that mounted on top of the pistons and this was called a "sneezer." The theory behind this was that when the injector sprayed diesel into the cylinder, it would hit this cone and cause the diesel fuel to spray out into a fine mist and evenly distribute it within the cylinder, and thereby get better combustion, sort of like a person sneezing, hence the name sneezers. Whether this improved anything or not I can't say, I do know that these little devices had a nasty habit of breaking off the piston inside the cylinder, and within a few revolutions of the motor, after this happened, the valves and pistons in that particular cylinder required a major overhaul. The lifetime of these sneezers was very short and I don't think there are very many left who recall them. These old engines also required special handling and driving, since they were a very low rpm engine running at approximately 1,600 rpm top end, and in dropping off a hill you had to keep the rpm at 1,400 or under If the engine was allowed, while under compression, to go to, say, 1,700 or 1,800 rpm, the top of the piston would make contact with a valve and leave a definite imprint of the valve on the top of the piston, and if allowed to go much over that speed, would end up damaging the cylinders. Also, in pulling a steep hill, if you applied full throttle to the engine, on a sustained pull the engine would get hot and seize up, seizing the rings against the cylinder walls. So you had to drop gears until you were in a range of power to keep from overworking the engine. In later engines, they installed a spray device that sprayed oil directly into the cylinder, thereby keeping it from overheating and seizing.

Another problem was that the sleeves they were putting into the cylinder block and shims were used to leave approximately 20 thousandths of an inch protruding above the surface of the block; then the head gasket was set down on the outside, thereby protecting the gasket. At least, that was the theory. It didn't work well at all, and we had many problems with head gaskets burning out, again causing the loss of valuable time. The cure for this was cylinder sleeves that had a fire ring circling the top outside the sleeves, and it worked really well. They faced the many things that befell them head-on, and the end result is today's trucks, fully loaded at 80,000 pounds or more, with the ability to keep up with traffic at speeds unheard of only a few years back. These trucks run fully computerized engines rated at 600 horsepower or more, at 1,200 to 2,100 rpm, for hundreds of thousands of miles, nearly full throttle at times with no damage—truly remarkable.

The evolution of brakes and braking systems over the years has been very interesting. From the very first days of transportation and using round wheels, there has been an ongoing challenge of controlling the speed of the horse-drawn wagon or motorized trucks on downhill grades. I recall my father hooking a chain around a big log and attaching it to the rear end of the hay wagon in order to descend steep hills on the coast of California with large loads of hay, to help hold the load back and not run over the teams of horses—rather a crude method, but it worked. When I first started hauling logs, we had a large tank mounted on the rear deck behind the cab and had water piped to all the brake drums, and upon dropping off these steep logging roads we turned the water on to run over the brake drums to keep them from overheating. It worked pretty well, and when used with the right speeds it made a much safer downhill trip for truck and driver. Another device they came up with was called a hydrotarder. It also worked with a supply of water; this device was in effect a water pump with two lines running into it from a supply tank on the rear of the cab. With the large pump affair mounted between the truck frame and the driveline running through the middle of it, the water entered through a large water inlet and discharged through a smaller outlet. This operated like a water pump in reverse and created back pressure on the driveline—this theoretically slowed the truck down, I always thought the theory was better than the practice. You could actually feel a slight slowing when it was first turned on, but after a short while it didn't seem to help much. I liked the water to the drums much better. The next thing they came up with was called a Williams exhaust brake. This was no more than a damper as used in a woodstove pipe; it was controlled by an air-operated switch from the truck cab and was placed inside the exhaust pipe close to where it came out of the manifold. When turning it on you could tell it was doing some good, but as with the rest of these devices, you had better drop off the hills at a slow rate of speed and continually hold the speed in check because these gadgets were not going to stop you if things got out of control.

With the invention of what is called the Jake brake, trucking suddenly took on another dimension. This marvel of ingenuity was invented by a man by the name of Clessie Cummins. If the name sounds familiar, it should. He is the same man who engineered the Cummins diesel engine. He sold his Cummins engine company and then went to work on developing the engine brake. After perfecting this system he went back to the company that had bought him out and offered them the first opportunity to manufacture and sell this device. They flat turned him down as their engineers claimed that if they used this it would destroy the engine. Clessie then approached the Jacobs engineering company and they immediately reached an agreement and started manufacturing this jewel called a Jake brake. Used throughout the trucking industry and on most every make and model of diesel engine, this device works by utilizing the cam shaft to control the opening and closing of the exhaust valves at the correct time resulting in a braking action for extremely efficient control of downhill speed, truly one of the best things to ever come along in the trucking industry. This device has saved untold amounts of money in the cost of replacing brake shoes and drums, not to mention the safety factor for truck and driver. This device was patented in 1965 and more than 1 ½ million units are installed on trucks, busses, and motorhomes worldwide. Caterpillar offers a retarder system that is used in addition to the Jake brake. This retarder is operated through the transmission and works very well. Using these devices together will take you off most every hill without ever touching your brakes.

The advent of the CB radio was certainly a very large help in the North—to be able to communicate with a truck coming toward you, letting each other know of animals, road conditions, of many and varied things—even more than in the South 48, where much of it is a lot of B.S. It was a real working tool in the Arctic North, and one that has saved many a wreck and probably saved people from being killed. We certainly always had a full complement on all our equipment of the very best antennas and CB radios that we could get. In later years they changed over in the North from CB to VHF broadcast band. It will get out 40 or 50 miles or more at times, especially in the North, and it is used almost exclusively in place of the CB radio. It is a wonderful, wonderful tool, and most truckers have it.

Another thing used up here that you won't find anywhere else because it is basically illegal, was aircraft landing lights. We used them when they first started putting them on, and they'd be mounted on top of the cab or along the bumper. These were highly illuminating lights, and the biggest problem with them was that through the rough roads and so forth they did not have a very long lifespan. They were rather expensive, but nonetheless we use them all the time to spot moose and other wildlife, because there is plenty of it here to contend with. They came out with a light that was perfected in Australia, called a light force. They are wonderful pieces of equipment, and they come in three different sizes. You can almost melt the ice on the road with them they're so bright, and basically all the trucks up here that run have them. They are a wonderful safety tool for protecting against running into moose and other wildlife. Most drivers will shut them off when meeting an oncoming rig. However, there are the select few that seem to love leaving them on to try and blind you, and that is exactly what happens. Thankfully this doesn't happen often.

To increase gross weight, truckers started using lift axles on tractors to make a four-axle rig out of a conventional three-axle truck. These axles were placed ahead of the drive axles, and were designed with a coil spring or leaf spring that actually lifts the wheels to clear the road approximately 6 inches when the air is released. The airbags are placed on top of the axles and with the application of air pressure, forces air into the bags, overcomes the spring action, and pushes the tires down to compact the road. These are controlled by the driver from within the cab by use of a trailer brake control handle moved by the driver that applies air pressure. The problem with this was that a driver could inadvertently set the handle too far and force an overload of air inside the bags and cause the steering axle to actually lift up the front axle enough to create a loss of steering ability, and on icy or slick roads could cause a driver to lose control. As an example, I recall an incident related to me by John Buck and Willey Willbanks who were with the heavy truck division of Alaska Sales and Service in Anchorage. They had a large delivery of trucks that came in on a ship at the docks out of Seattle; these were some of the very first with the new lift axles to arrive in Alaska. They went together to pick up one of these rigs and on the way back Willey was driving and John was experimenting with the lift axle and applied far too much air pressure. When they came to a red stoplight Willey stepped on the brakes; however, because of the lack of weight on the tractor, the drive axles had risen completely off the road and with no brakes on the lift axle, Willey had his foot pressing as hard as he could on the brake pedal, but without the drive axles on the pavement they were without any brake power whatsoever through the red light. Fortunately, they didn't meet any other vehicles within the intersection. Another incident occurred with a lift axle that didn't have such a happy ending. When a driver was pulling Long Lake hill in the early 1970s, the roads were terrible and traction was very bad, and in conditions such as these the driver would release the air and raise the lift axle, thereby allowing more weight to apply to the drive axles, resulting in better traction. After he had reached the top of the hill, he apparently applied too much air pressure to the lift axles, and being heavy on the fifth wheel, it raised or reduced the weight on the front steering axles, the truck was unable to negotiate the next corner, went to the bottom of the canyon, and he was killed. I was just a short way behind him at the time.

After several incidents of this nature, the control valves in the cab were set up to keep the driver from exceeding the recommended air pressure to the lift axles, thereby reducing accidents as described above. Alaska has since talked about making the use of lift axles illegal, because drivers used them going through the scales, and after getting out of sight of the scales would lift them up, adding several pounds of weight to the drive axles, which of course gave better traction The state didn't like the idea of the drive axles allowing drivers to exceed the legal limits, so at one time they were getting pretty serious about trying to outlaw them, but they are still being used.

I was driving an old cab equipped with an air throttle out of Glennallen, hauling fuel. I guess the rationale behind it was that you could not run the engine faster than at idle speed when cold-starting until you had at least 30 to 40 pounds of air pressure built up. This throttle worked very well until it gave up on me one day down at Chitna, Alaska. I could get the engine to run only at idle speed. Anyway, I finally raised the cab, took an air line off from where the connections were down by the end of the steering wheel shaft, and got the air line from the trailer brake control. I isolated that and switched it over to the throttle line, where it came out of the foot throttle, and each time I pulled on the trailer brake handle, I could rev the engine up. It worked very well. I could totally control the engine speed by the amount of pressure that was applied to the brake handle. So I figured I would drive it back to Anchorage and get it fixed. Well, I pulled into Mark Moore's shop in Anchorage and told Mark what I needed, and he laughed and said, "Cliff, I only know of one other rig in the whole state that still uses that setup, but I'll order one for you out of the South 48." So I figured, what the heck, I made it into town with the brake handle so I'll just run it back the same way. It was quite an experience, shifting a five-speed main and a four-speed auxiliary while revving the engine up and down with the hand-operated throttle. However, I got quite adept at it, since it took at least two weeks to locate and get the part sent to Anchorage. So I made at least a dozen more trips with that makeshift arrangement. After Mark got it fixed for me, I was headed back to Glennallen and there was ice on the road. It was very slick. I was using my Jake brake and dropping off the hill, and as it happens on occasion the engine started to die from the Jake brake setting up the drivers. I always either shut the Jake brake switch off or just hit the throttle. Well, after all the hand throttle stuff I had been doing, I quick as a flash reached up and pulled the hand throttle on—but instead of the throttle, I set the brakes to the trailer, and I was in big trouble. The engine quit dead and the brakes started sliding the trailer wheels. I got it straightened out, got the engine started back up and straightened up without going off the road, but I never again pulled that brake handle for the throttle after that little episode.

Chapter Twelve
Summer and Midnight Sun

The extreme cold of winter behind us and going into spring has always been a welcome relief to me. Looking forward to the long summer days ahead and the many activities that took place over the summer months: weekend getaways, midnight ball games, fishing, barbecues, just being able to function without wearing several layers of cold-weather gear was always a blessing. Although the days are getting longer, you can just about bet that around March the weather will take a nasty turn for a few days of subzero temperatures, and snow flurries up into April, and occasionally into May. I recall the date of May 18. I was on a trip into Anchorage to pick up fuel, and after I left Glennallen and arrived at Eureka, 60 miles down the road, it was snowing and about 2 or 3 inches had accumulated on the roads. It was very sloppy, for the roadbeds were not frozen down as they are in winter. So being a savvy driver, I watched my drive tires and trailer tires out the rearview mirror, and by the spray mixture of snow and water knew that the traction was okay. I got on down the road a few miles to Caribou Canyon, a short but steep hill that had a record of many wrecked trucks over the years. So with my being an expert, I simply slowed down to about 20 miles an hour and broke over the top of the hill. I was driving a tanker truck and a pull trailer. Well, I got approximately 150 to 200 feet down the hill and all the wheels on the truck and trailer lost traction. This part of the road was in the shade and still frozen. My pull trailer was trying its best to pass me up. I got around the first turn and tried my best to put the whole outfit into the ditch on the right side, the upside of the road, since on the left there was a very steep canyon. Try as I might I could not get far enough over to do this and all the time I was picking up speed and doing everything in my power to keep this out-of-control rig on the road. About every 100 feet I was looking over my left side straight down the steep hill to the riverbed below and somehow managed to keep from going over. I made the decision to jump out and let the whole outfit go. I opened the door and the trailer was sliding sideways and would run over me if I jumped, so back to wrestling with the steering wheel, brakes, and throttle. I somehow stayed on the road, and hitting the right-hand shoulder several times kept the speed down enough for me to make it onto the bridge at the bottom of the hill, where I got it stopped. After sitting for a few minutes to try and regain my composure I got out and put chains on in order to get up the other side. Approximately three quarters of a mile to the top of the hill I took the chains

Summer time in Alaska.

off, since the snow there was melting, and I went on into Anchorage. Coming back in about five and a half, six hours I found the road wet but without any snow visible. So Alaska has its own way of keeping you humbled when you think you know it all.

One of the big events in the springtime is the Nenana Ice Classic. They set up a tripod in the middle of the river with a line from the top of it over to the shore, and that records the hour and minute that the ice moves. People make bets on the exact day and time and minute that it breaks up and turns the tripod over. This happens most often in late April or May but in certain years it happened much sooner and later, so these guesses cover many months and

24 hours around the clock. In spite of Alaska's and the Yukon's reputation of being the last frontier with rip-roaring saloons, dance hall girls, and booze, this Ice Classic is the only form of gambling allowed in the state, with the exception of a few bingo halls and scratch tickets. Las Vegas and Reno are very happy over this fact, because they reap many Alaska dollars from the North Slope workers and residents who travel to Nevada for some fun and games with their pocket full of hard-earned money. It is beyond me why we are not allowed this form of entertainment without even a lottery to play in a state that was renowned for its unrestricted way of life.

By the time the longest day of the year arrives in June, we've always tried to arrange a midnight softball game in Glennallen, starting at about 11 p.m. and going throughout the midnight hour under the light of the midnight sun. It was always a fun thing ending up with beer drinking, barbecues, bragging rights as to who won the game. The summers are such a fun thing in Alaska—waking up in the morning with sunlight and going to bed with the sun still shining. Kind of hard to get used to when you first arrive from the South 48. I was always intrigued by the kids playing baseball, basketball, football, or other endeavors at 12, 1, and 2 a.m. or later, totally oblivious to the time on the clock and just having a great time. This all-night daylight is also used extensively by the fishermen. When you drive past the end of the fishing streams they are always well attended by these avid fishermen, at all hours around the clock. The residents of the South 48 have watched the sun come up in the east and set in the western sky all their lives. It is a rare sight in the winter months in Alaska to see the sun rise in the southeast just about 10 a.m. and then move along the southern horizon and set in the southwest about one or two o'clock in the afternoon, never rising much above the southern horizon on the shortest days of the year. In the far north of Alaska, it never gets up in sight at all during this time. In the longest days of summer, the sun rises in the northeast, and sets in the northwest, dipping just below the horizon and again on the longest days and in the farthest north part of Alaska does not dip under the horizon at all. This is therefore known as the land of the midnight sun. It takes a newcomer a while to get used to this, but I believe most people learn to look forward to these super-long summer days. I certainly do. However, there is a price to pay for these long days and that price is the short days of winter. For every long day of summer there is a corresponding short day of winter. I have always believed that the visitors to our fair land in the summer, who come north and enjoy these never-ending days of daylight, should have to spend equal time in the winter to understand the price we residents pay for this never-ending sunshine.

Chapter Thirteen
Alaska's Inhabitants: Wolves, Bears, and Characters

During one of my periods of work between driving jobs, I was involved at the old Rosents café at the corner of the Glenn and Richardson highways in Glennallen, as a one-third owner and manager of the service station. One of my partners hired a young man who was hitchhiking through the area, and he ended up working for me in the service station. After he had worked there a few days, I found out that he was from Cottonwood, California, a little town 5 miles from where I lived in Anderson, California, just north of there. He knew several people I'd known there. He was not a great worker, and I got on him pretty hard several times for things that he was told to do and for his treatment of some of the customers. I think in looking back that the only reason why he stayed on was that we had a huge old iron safe where we kept the cash receipts from the café and the service station until we were able to take them to the bank. It seems that every time I opened the safe, this young man was standing behind me looking over my shoulder. I finally told him that if I caught him doing this again I would wring his neck for him, because it was obvious he was trying to get the combination of the safe. There were several incidents of cash missing from the till, and I finally gave him his walking papers. About three months later I found out that he had killed five people prior to working for me, two of whom I had known in Anderson, California—an old couple who owned and operated the Bluebird Motel just north of Anderson. Apparently, he shot them during an attempted robbery. He then went to Kodiak, Alaska and killed a woman and her two children and burned their house up. After leaving Glennallen he killed two traveling salesmen who had given him rides as he was hitchhiking to Louisiana, where he was caught. I often think back to my experience and exposure to this madman and consider myself very fortunate not to have ended up as one of his victims.

After being involved in the service station for a short while I decided to start a grocery store in the old abandoned bar located next to the cafe and service station. This was another new experience and a lot of fun. It worked very well and was such a success that a young man from Anchorage who was employed by a big grocery chain, Carr-Gottstien, came to Glennallen and wanted to buy me out as he could see the potential for this fledgling business, I had decided by this time that I was not cut out to be a grocer for the rest of my life so let him have it, this man was Park Kriner, He ran this grocery store at it's original site for a while and then started expanding. Today, if you are going through Glennallen, you will probably be doing business with Park as he now owns a large grocery store, Parks Place Omni Grocery and also Caribou Motel and Cafe.

There's a man who had a cabin on the Tok Cutoff, which connects the Richardson Highway out of Glennallen to Tok on the Alaska Highway. This man was known as the Mad Trapper, and his cabin was near Mentasta. A gentleman from Glennallen, Irving Hockstadter, a family man who had five or six children, had the contract to deliver mail from Glennallen to Tok. One day he stopped in at this trapper's cabin, which was located about 100 yards off the main road, to tell the trapper that if he put up a mailbox in front of his place they would drop the mail off there instead of having to make the trapper go into Tok on occasion to pick up his mail, 30 or 40 miles up the road. In any event, Irving was walking up toward the cabin and the trapper came out with a 3:06 and shot him, killed him dead, then walked over on the highway and put three or four bullet holes in his truck besides. Well, come to find out this trapper had killed a person several years before and had been put into a mental institution, where he'd spent three or four years, and they had released him back to his cabin. This was a totally unprovoked act, and again the trapper ended up being declared insane. And I couldn't believe it—about four years after this I was going toward Tok in the truck and guess who was walking down the road? The Mad Trapper. They had let him out again and although I never heard of him shooting anyone else, I always watched both sides of the road when I was in that vicinity, and was darn careful that he didn't have me in his sights.

And of course, another infamous character was one at McCarthy in the Wrangell Mountains, a man by the name of Hastings. This man had a grudge against the construction of an oil pipeline running through the state ending in Valdez, and he decided he was going to blow it up. McCarthy is located in the mountains a long ways from the pipeline and, of course, to try and make sense out of his actions would be impossible, since he'd obviously gone off the deep end. In any event, what he did was start killing the residents of this little mountain village, and according to the story he told after the fact, his intentions were to kill all the residents, some 15 or so people, then hijack the mail plane that came in every few days, fly down to the Richardson Highway, commandeer one of my big tankers, rig it with explosives and blow up pump station # 12 on the Richardson Highway. The mail plane pilot, Lynn Ellis, was coming in to land, and looked down and saw some people who appeared to be dead lying on or near the runway. He aborted his landing and radioed the state troopers. When they arrived in their helicopter, Hastings was on a snowmachine trying to escape, and they hovered over him with their guns pointed down. He decided to give up and they took him into custody. This whole episode was so bizarre. I knew most of these folks that were killed, since they came in to our bulk plant in Glennallen to purchase oil and gas products, so this goes on and on. There are a lot of backwoods people who think they can get away with whatever.

Another incident that comes to mind is the Mendeltna Lodge on the Glenn Highway. The wife of the lodge owner there had disappeared, and several people in the area had been told that she had gone on a vacation. Well, they pretty well knew that this didn't happen and anyway, after a month or so the state troopers got involved. There was a dump area near the lodge, a public dump, and they found a fire pit there and some bone in it. Someone put two and two together and they took samples of these bones, and sure enough they were human bones. The end result was that he claimed that he had gotten in a fight with her, she had fallen and hit her head on the edge of the metal stool, and it killed her. He had burned her up because he was afraid that because of his prison record they would think he was a murderer, which I believe he was. Anyway, he got away with this. They never did prosecute him for murder. They gave him some jail time, but it was for manslaughter or something along those lines. So much again for Alaska backwoods justice. Sometimes they just don't get it.

Another situation pretty much along the same lines was that of an old man by the name of Simon Jensen who lived on the Nelchina River, again on the Glenn Highway. There was a trapper there who lived in a dilapidated old cabin, and he had an about 13- or 14-year-old daughter living there with him. It was kind of a strange setup and I had this feeling of total mistrust about the trapper. I had met him at the café several times and he came across as a definite nutcase. I even talked to Phyllis McGinley, who owned the Nelchina Café, since I was of the opinion that this man was not to be trusted, especially since Phyllis and Frank McGinley were taking care of their three grandkids, Kim, Roxanne, and Blake Beaudoin. I told Phyllis that I thought this guy was capable of most anything and not to trust him, especially with these kids around. I think Phyllis took me seriously, since she also had an uncomfortable feeling of mistrust about him, and stated as much. I would see them walking on the road—they lived about a half mile from Simon's place—and I'd see them walking to or from his cabin. Simon had lived at his Nelchina River cabin for several years, a very friendly man, and waved to me when I was going to and from Anchorage to pick up fuel. I would also see him at the café as he walked up there for coffee, and to visit on a regular basis, and one morning I saw all three of them walking on the road near Simon's cabin, and as usual, Simon gave me a big friendly wave. I didn't see him again for several days and since he always went to the café for coffee, well, Phyllis got concerned when he didn't show up for about four or five days. The state trooper stopped by there and she mentioned it to him. They got to checking and they couldn't find hide nor hair of him. I stopped by on my way to Anchorage, and they asked me if I had seen him. I told them I had seen the three of them walking there on a particular day. I recalled vividly that I had seen them and what day it was. But anyway, through the questioning and everything, the daughter finally told the troopers that indeed her father had killed Simon and they'd wrapped him up in blankets and hauled him in Simon's old pickup down to the Knik River bridge near Palmer, and thrown his body over the bridge into the Knik River. Anyway, they arrested the trapper and put the daughter in protective custody, and into somebody's house or whatever. Anyway, she managed to disappear within a week or so and they never did find her. Last I heard was that they had to let the guy go because they had no witness; it was just hearsay, and no body, and they never did prosecute him for this murder. They knew he was a murderer but they had no way of proving it. So again, sometimes some strange things have happened in the backwoods of Alaska. I heard later that this man was caught in California robbing a jewelry store and was in prison .

Lotti Sparks was a lady who lived in Glennallen and worked for me as a bookkeeper for a period of time. She bought a lodge on the Glenn Highway, situated next to a lake called Tex Smith Lake. This lodge was built by Tex Smith and his son, Perry—nothing out of the ordinary, except the son went on to become an infamous murderer and was one of the two men who killed the whole Clutter family in Kansas and was the basis for Truman Capote's book *In Cold Blood*. A movie was made by the same name. An old-timer by the name of Cliff Steadman hauled the mail from Anchorage to Glennallen and told me that Perry, the son, used to wait for him and ride the last 20 or so miles into Glennallen, and then get off back at the lodge on his return. Cliff said he was totally surprised by what the kid had done, as he was a real like-able boy and he could not imagine him being part of such a heinous crime. It was interesting to go through the old lodge and see some of the reminders of their past presence. Obviously, Tex Smith got his nickname from his home state of Texas and I guess that's why there were six or eight rattlesnake skins still up on the walls. The kid had also carved his initials in some of the logs, P.S. for Perry Smith. I saw the movie and just being in this place where he had lived brought back thoughts of the horror of what this person had done in killing that whole family for absolutely nothing; as I recall they only took a few dollars away from the scene of this senseless crime.

There was a man in Anchorage who was an avid hunter and pilot, and was famous for taking a world-record Dall sheep with a bow and arrow. He also owned a bakery shop, and when not in his bake shop or out in his airplane on a hunting trip, he spent a large amount of time at the local strip clubs in Anchorage. It came to the attention of the Anchorage Police Department that over a period of one or two years, a lot of the dancing girls and prostitutes were missing, for their friends and coworkers made missing-persons reports. It didn't raise too many red flags initially, because these girls traveled into and out of Anchorage to Fairbanks and even to Seattle and other South 48 locations, and sometimes left on the spur of the moment. However, over a period of time the sheer number of these reports did indeed get the attention of authorities and raised their suspicions that something could possibly be happening to these girls, and a full-scale investigation was started. This went on for quite some time, with even more girls disappearing regularly. Police were unable to locate them or get any leads in the mystery until in the early-morning hours a young lady was spotted running naked down Fifth Avenue in Anchorage, adjacent to the local airport, and upon being picked up by a passing motorist and taken to the police department told them that a man had coerced her into his car after she got off work at one of the clubs, and had forced her to take off all her clothes, then drove her to the airport. In the process of getting her from the car into the airplane, she'd broken away and run out into the street, which was just a short distance from where the planes were tied down. With this incident, the police got their big break and in the ensuing investigation, after searching his home, found a large stash of neck-laces, rings, and other jewelry he had kept as souvenirs of his nefarious deeds. After finding all this evidence, and with the naked girl's testimony, they were certain they had the person responsible for all the missing girls. After further interrogation, the police finally got to the details of how these girls had disappeared and how and where they ended up. The man, whose first name was Bob, and by this time was known as Bad Bob the Baker, had persuaded the girls to leave the club with him by promising money, airplane rides, or other things. In any event, when he got to his car, he would overpower them, tie them up, take them to the plane and force them into it at gunpoint, and then fly the Alaska bush plane with its oversized tires that allowed him to land on gravel and sandbars, to the Knik River a few miles out of Anchorage. At that point, after landing, he would release the girl and taking his weapon of choice, a bow and arrow or a gun, tracked down his released quarry and killed her. He then dug a very shallow grave and buried her there. This catch-and-release went on over twenty-five times, possibly more, and only by pure luck, by one of the girls escaping when she did, a stop was put to this serial killer. This man was seen at home mowing his lawn or taking off in the family car with his wife and family and did not give anyone a clue as to the monster he was. I observed this man many times—he was our neighbor in Anchorage, and our kids were playmates with his children. He invited me to go hunting with him, and although I never went I have often wondered if on getting me out into the back country with no women around he might have used me for target practice. And even this man did not get the death sentence for all of these atrocities, although he is serving life behind bars.

Cliff Steadman had the mail contract between Glennallen and Palmer. He and his son Clive were headed up the road to Glennallen; he had a little eating area set up in the back of his mail truck, and carried a few groceries along to fix a light lunch, because this trip lasted 9 or 10 hours. They would stop at the pullout on the road about halfway to Glennallen, and went back to get a bite to eat, and pulled one of the doors closed after getting inside. It was rather chilly. They were sitting there eating when all of a sudden they realized that the door lever was being locked from the outside. At first Cliff thought one of his friends was playing a trick on him but after a half hour or more he knew otherwise. They stayed locked up in the back of the truck for almost two hours before a friend came along and recognized his rig, and stopped to see what was wrong with the mail truck. Upon stopping, he was greeted by a loud hammering on the van walls and loud yelling. What had happened was that two guys came up on the stopped truck and in walking by the cab, saw Cliff's wallet sitting on the seat. Realizing that he was in the back end, they locked the door and grabbed the wallet and went on up the road. Just as they were pulling back on the road for their getaway, another acquaintance of Cliff's drove by and saw the car and upon finding out what had happened, gave the troopers a description. They were caught several hours later outside Fairbanks. Cliff said he didn't stop eating in the back of his truck because of this, but always locked up the cab and put the wallet out of sight after that.

Another old-timer, by the name of Jack Wallace, who was well known throughout Alaska trucking circles, always liked his drinking and was a frequent visitor to many of the bars in Alaska. One night in Anchorage, Jack had been out partying and in the early morning hours got back to his truck, which was parked near the top of a hill on Fourth Avenue. He got in the truck and undressed and crawled into the sleeper, and for whatever reason, nobody knows, the truck ran down the hill and without hitting anything, stopped in an awkward position in a snowbank. At the same time a TV news mobile unit was going by returning from a house fire they had covered, and on seeing the red lights of the cop cars that were rushing to the scene, they stopped and cranked up their cameras when out of the sleeper came Jack and the cops, who were in the process of trying to arrest him for drunk driving, Jack was dressed in no more than his shorts and was about to be arrested for this transgression, all of which appeared on the six-o'clock news. I don't think Jack ever outlived the ribbing he took over that incident. He was finally exonerated of any wrongdoing.

Another thing I observed was Jack's vehicle parked in front of several different bars with the horn blowing. The first time I noticed this I went over by his car and inside were two small dogs who were jumping up on the steering wheel, causing the horn to blow. I thought this was just a coincidence until I saw the same thing happen several other times until Jack came out of the bar. Jack told the story of a homesteader friend of his who lived outside Tok in a small two-room cabin. He had three kids, so it was quite cramped. Jack was visiting one time and said he noticed a large jar of Vaseline sitting on the floor by the bedroom door. In the course of the conversation, Jack asked, "What is that jar for?" The friend kind of hesitated and said with a little grin on his face, "Well, with no locks on the door and the kids not giving us any privacy, we put Vaseline on the doorknob so when we're in there making out the kids can't get in." A rather novel way of handling a delicate situation.

A lot of drivers put a name on the side of their trucks—you've probably all seen them, probably after their wives, kids, girlfriends, whatever. Sally, Jane, Sue. One of the more unique things I recall was that a friend of mine, Harry Banahan, and two partners started a little freight delivery business running from Anchorage to Whittier, a town just south of Anchorage. It was accessible in those days only by train; it went from Anchorage down to the Whittier docks' train depot loading ramp. They loaded the vehicles on the train and went over to Whittier through the tunnels, hauling supplies in there a couple of times a week. They had bought this truck, a box van, as a delivery rig. In any event, on the side of the truck it spelled out as bold as could be, "M-O-N" and then a space, "G-O," space, "W-A-R." This truck became quite a unique thing. People in Whittier referred to the fact that old Mon-go-war would arrive with supplies today, tomorrow, or whenever. This truck had been a Montgomery Ward delivery truck and with the letters missing out of it, spelled the perfect Mon-go-war. We got quite a chuckle out of it.

This book would not be complete without adding this piece about my old friend Scatter Edwards, a World War II vetern, avid patriot, and well known bar owner who operated the Rainbow Lodge in Wasilla on the Parks Highway,. Having spent most of the war as an aerial gunner he had very little respect for the enemy even after it was over. One day a group of Japanese tourists stopped in at his Lodge and one of them asked in broken English "where Mt McKinley?" With a typical Scatter Edwards response he said, "you damn Japs found Pearl Harbor in the fog in the middle of the Pacific—just go out in front on the highway and look up to your right!" This man was a legend in his own time and was a never ending source of entertainment.

Chapter Fourteen
Drivers' Stories

What is known as the Glory Hole, located on the Richardson Highway between Paxson and Delta Junction, is an area of legendary winds. Trucks have been stranded there for days at a time with travel through there being impossible during the high winds and drifting snow.

Vic Unfer had gone to Hawaii and got married and spent a couple of weeks on the Hawaiian Islands on his honeymoon. Upon returning he went to Valdez, picked up a load of fuel on his first trip back, and headed toward Fairbanks. Upon reaching the Glory Hole area, it caught him up in one of these ferocious storms and he was caught there for over two days before road equipment was able to reach his truck. Vic didn't have any food whatsoever on this trip and he said that never again would he be caught with no emergency rations after this experience.

I have had my hood blown over and up in front of my face going down the road at 30 or 40 miles an hour in the same direction the winds were blowing, and had the wind blow hard enough to break or pull loose the rubber hold-down straps that hold the hood down, and tip it up in the air so I couldn't see the road. What a hell of a time I had getting it tipped back down and secure enough to go on down the road. There was also a state road grader working in this area one winter and he had a native Indian boy with him when one of the big winds came up and they were stuck for many hours waiting for the storm to stop. After they had sat there for hours on end, it was getting pretty critical, and the boy asked the operator what they could do. "Pray," he replied. So the kid, who had been tutored by missionaries in the area, dropped to his knees, and said, "Please God, come and get us. You come yourself, don't send your kid. We're in big trouble." The grader operator said it absolutely worked because soon after the wind died and road equipment came and rescued them.

I recall going to Anchorage from Glennallen one morning, and several spots in the road had some heavy-duty frost heaves—that meant if you hit a bump it would propel you to the roof of the truck if you weren't careful. I hit one down by Mendeltna Creek and the air ride seat went up in the air. I went up in the air with it and came back down and all of a sudden the whole cab disappeared in front of my eyes. What had happened is that I had come down on a fire extinguisher that was underneath the seat of the truck. It activated the fire extinguisher and almost immediately filled the cab with a thick white cloud. I rolled the window down as fast as I could and stuck my head out, all the while getting on the brakes. I got stopped before I ran off the road, but I tell you, that was quite a rude awakening. From that time on, I made certain that the extinguisher was properly stored.

I recall a driver who drove for LTI, Lynden Transport, who went by the first name of Glenn. We used to run across each other frequently on the road, usually at Eureka Lodge, and we were talking one day about cabovers versus conventional cab rigs. He made the statement that given the choice, no way would he drive the cabover, I asked what his big problem was, since I was running a cabover at that time and thought it was a pretty good rig. Glenn said that several years before he'd been driving a cabover across one of the Midwest states on a flat stretch of road that seemed to go on forever, when he went sound asleep and woke up with his truck lying flat on its right side. Of course, Glenn was wide awake by this time and scrambling to get up out of the cab, all the while checking for blood, broken bones, and so forth, and feeling pretty good that nothing seemed to be wrong. He got up to the driver's side window, stood up on the door, and stepped on the wheel in order to scramble onto the ground. Remember, this was a cabover. When stepping onto the front wheel, he got flung into the air and about 15 feet away from the truck to the ground because the wheel was still turning at approximately 45 to 50 miles per hour. The end result was a broken leg and wrist when he hit the ground. So now I understood why he had a thing against driving a cabover. And the only thing I can say about it is if you are driving a cabover, don't go to sleep.

I had a driver on the local delivery truck, Richard Schultz, who had a Samoyed, a white sled dog, and he was out delivering fuel to residents in the Glennallen area, when this dog ran underneath the truck while he was unloading. The power takeoff was in gear and apparently the dog's tail, which he held up in the air all the time over his back, caught up into the power shaft on the power takeoff and tragically tore the hide off his back. It rolled it up on the shaft and the dog ran out from underneath the truck, still alive, with all his hide missing off his back and ran off into the woods. This poor guy had nightmares over this. They never did find that dog. It ran off and, of course, died or was killed by a coyote or wolf or whatever. He had nightmares over this thing and I can certainly understand why. At a later date, another company there had the same situation on these fuel pumps. They would leak some time in the packing gland, and if you got underneath and got a crescent wrench and tightened up a couple of bolts, it would put pressure against the packing and would stop the leaking as you were pumping product off the truck. Well, unfortunately this young man got his coat sleeve tied up in the power takeoff—there's a little set screw in there, and evidently this hooked into the sleeve on his coat when he was doing this and absolutely wrapped him up in a ball. I talked to the fellows who removed him and they were traumatized by this tragic accident.

Three or four drivers were sitting in the 101 Café in Copper Center, right alongside the Richardson Highway, and one of the guys, Bob Growden, was headed down to Valdez to pick up a load and was empty, of course. He left there and in probably 10, 12 minutes his truck came back from the Valdez direction. We knew there was no place to turn around that close to Copper Center. This was a narrow, two-lane road and probably 20 feet across max, and yet there he was, sitting there. What had happened was that there was a grader across the road and in the heavy snow he got up so close that he would have hit it if he hadn't stopped, or jackknifed, so he hit his brakes and the whole outfit very neatly turned around within the confines of this narrow two-lane road It swung around behind him and he ended up completely turned around and headed back toward Copper Center. It didn't hurt anything other than a slight bend in the trailer tongue. When he first got there and we asked what had happened, he said that he had simply forgotten his lunch bucket, so decided to turn around and come back and pick it up. He said this is not a very difficult thing to do if you knew what you were doing. It was very funny, and we laughed a lot about it.

Another of the many truck driver stories I recall was about my old friend Bob Cavalero. We were in Mark Moore's shop in Anchorage when Bob came in after he had just taken delivery on his brand-new Kenworth with a V-12 jimmy engine in it. It was one of the biggest engines around at the time. In the course of the bull session going on, one of the guys who was driving a rig with a 200 hp engine said to Bob, "I could beat you to Fairbanks by two hours, driving the same weight load and everything being equal." Bob asked, "How the hell is a two-hundred hp rig going to beat my V-12 into Fairbanks?" The guy said, "Well, Bob, I would just hire a new waitress and put her to work at the Paxson Lodge on the way to Fairbanks, and I'm thinking you will be tied up with her for at least two hours while I'm going on up the road." We all got a big kick out of this, because everyone knew Bob's reputation for being the romantic type. He really liked to BS the waitresses. He was a real nice guy and all the waitresses enjoyed his company. This was the Bob Cavalero we all knew and loved.

We were hauling fuel out of the Union Oil plant in Anchorage 24 hours per day. Union Oil didn't want to keep personnel there, so they gave me keys to unlock the plant gates and tanks. It was a simple matter of going in and just recording the loads we picked up. They kept the main tanks locked, across the street from the loading docks of the Union Oil company. One night I went in there with another couple of trucks. I was up on the load rack filling up with diesel, and gave one of the other drivers the keys to unlock and turn the valves on the big gasoline tanks over across the road. Well, I looked over there and I could not believe my eyes. There was a fire going. I jumped down and ran as hard as I could and out of breath, I got over there. As I got closer I saw that the driver had a fire going underneath the locked valve on this huge gasoline tank He had taken a newspaper out of his truck and lit a fire underneath the lock, which was iced up, to thaw it out. I could not believe the stupidity of this individual. I got the thing put out in hurry. It did the job, but it also almost gave me a heart attack on seeing it. They would have kicked me out of there—I would never have hauled another load if they had found out. On another occasion in Anchorage, I had a couple of trucks leased to Copper Freight Lines, Leonard Wilbanks and John Buck, a whole bunch of them there—Skip Weeks, Dayton Prince. In any event, I went by the yard one evening in my car. It was about five o'clock in the afternoon. Pete Wiley, the dispatcher, and all of them were out standing in the street, when I looked over and saw one of my trucks, my brand-new cabover Freightliner, pulling out into the street. He was dragging the rear axle, so I drove over there and the guy stopped. I crawled up on the side, and told him there was a release button over there, to push that button in. I asked him where he was headed with the tractor, and he said, "Well, my rig broke down at Eagle River so I asked the dispatcher to borrow this rig to go out and pull my trailer on in." He said they gave him the green light. I told him to just push the button in and release the brakes, which he did, and then he took off. Well, about eleven o'clock that night I got a call at home and the driver who was supposed to pick the truck up had called the dispatcher wondering where the truck was. They called me and I said I saw a guy pull it out of there who said he had borrowed it. Well, Pete Wiley didn't know anything about it and the guy obviously stole the truck. The end result of it was that we didn't find the truck for about three days. This guy was going in and out of the military base over at Fort Rich. He was a GI and he kept telling the gate guards that he went to pick his trailer up and it wasn't ready and they hadn't unloaded it. Finally, one guy had seen him three or four times and decided his story was B.S., so he stopped him and found out that the truck was stolen. And the guy had run over a woman's foot in a crosswalk and almost killed her, hit a pickup and ran from that. It was a terrible situation that could have been a lot worse, because he was not a truck driver. Anyway, they caught him, and I guess he probably got dishonorably discharged and all kinds of repercussions over it, but it was quite a deal, and it came to pass that I had helped the guy steal my own truck. I got reminded of it many times.

I had a driver by the name of Marvin Glaze, who was on a regular run from Anchorage to Glennallen almost daily. He used to stop up at Eureka Lodge There was a good-looking waitress there, and Marvin being the type of individual that he was, tried to get her to go out with him. Unfortunately for me, her boyfriend was a state trooper. So Marvin was in there telling her that if her boyfriend gave him any trouble, I was going to have him sent to the North Slope to pull duty up there. I never made that statement, and there's nothing further from the truth, but I started getting all kinds of hassles from the trooper relating to equipment violations and driver's logs and things like that. It got to the point that a day didn't go by that one of the trucks didn't get stopped and get ticketed for something or other. I couldn't prove that it was harassment. Then one day I got a call about 9 a.m. A trucker was tied up at Eureka Lodge and I asked what the problem was. He told me it was a bad front tire and the trooper said it was too dangerous to drive on the highway with it. So I loaded up a new tire and headed to Eureka. When I got there, nothing was wrong with the tire. Nonetheless, I changed the tire and then my driver went on to Anchorage. I had witnesses to the fact that I had changed the tire, and Hal, the guy that owned the lodge there, verified it. I went back to Glennallen and talked to the head trooper there and told him this guy was doing a number on me. He said he didn't think the guy would do that. I said I could prove he had and he asked me how and I got the tire out of the back and explained that I had just changed it from the truck. The tire was up and had air in it and looked fine. He said, "I don't see anything wrong with it." I replied that I didn't think there could be, considering the fact that I had picked that truck up brand-new off the barge from Seattle and loaded it with the very first load it had ever hauled in Anchorage yesterday. When stopped by the trooper, it had less than 300 total miles on it, and it was on its way back into town this morning and these were brand-new tires. That pretty much proved that there was nothing wrong with this truck or the tire and it was a bunch of B.S. The end result was that I told the head trooper that if there were any more problems I would file charges. Needless to say, we didn't become close friends with the trooper, but I got my point across and we were never bothered again by this individual.

Another trooper story that comes to mind was a situation involving a driver who was having an affair with a trooper's wife. However, the driver's wife found out about it and caught them making out inside a pickup camper the driver owned, which she had found out was used regularly for these meetings. The wife had an extra key for the truck—she sneaked up and put a padlock on the camper door and then proceeded to drive the truck over to the trooper's house and backed it up to the front porch, at which point she blew the horn and then strolled out to the street, where her friend, who had taken her to the secret meeting site, was waiting. She got in the car and drove away. I never found out the outcome of this episode but always wondered what it was.

There was a driver by the name of Meyers, known as Chrome Dome for the lack of hair on his head. He was on his way back to Anchorage from Fairbanks and ran off the road when hitting black ice near Sourdough on the Richardson Highway. His truck ran almost 100 yards out into the willow trees and these little trees didn't break off—they just bent over and then popped back up after you passed over them. You couldn't even see his truck from the road. They pulled it out by a different path than it had entered, so there really was no way of telling that anything had ever been in there. One of Chrome's friends, a fellow driver, painted a good-sized sign and nailed it on a tree. It said "Chrome Dome's Hideaway." The sign stayed there for several years. I don't think he appreciated it very much but the rest of us got a kick out of it.

Jim Stepp, a longtime Alaskan driver, bought a pull trailer from me back in the Pipeline days. I don't even remember what the deal was, but he somehow figured that he still owed me $500 on it. This happened in 1979 or '80 and in 1996 he made a special effort to look me up and gave me a check for $500. I never met too many people as honest as Jim.

I was working in the shop for Bayless and Roberts in Copper Center, when a driver came in after hauling a load to Valdez complaining how bad his truck was running. The load was sent down from Anchorage and was marked as a high priority. He said that it seemed to be fine on his way down but lost a lot of power on the return back to Copper Center, in particular pulling the big hill up over Thompson Pass. He said that the truck ran so bad that he figured the fuel filters were plugged up. This came as a surprise to us, for we had just serviced this rig a day or two earlier. We told him to go have a cup of coffee at the 101 Café and we would check it out. We had a couple of trucks in the shop, so we had to get one of them out before pulling his rig in. After about 45 minutes the dispatcher came over to the shop looking for the driver. The people in Valdez had called and wanted to know where the hell their load was. The driver had pulled into their yard in Valdez and left his truck and loaded van, had then gone with one of his buddies for a bite to eat. He'd come back and taken off, still loaded. The truck's power problem was solved.

Charley Barr tells about the trucker who got his first truck and had a contract hauling from Anchorage to Fairbanks, well after six months of hard running he came out almost $4,000 short, so this same company had an opening for another truck on the excact same haul so the guy goes out and buys another truck to make up for his lost revenue with the first one; well Charley mulled this over after being told of what had transpired and came up with this comment "the guy really knows how to truck, but he sure as hell dose'nt understand arithmetic."

Chapter Fifteen
Accidents

Over the years, when running on the roads in Alaska and the Arctic North, one thing that every company can rely on is the call that one of its trucks is off the road or was involved in an accident. These calls can result from road conditions so bad that it becomes impossible to stand up, let alone operate a fully loaded rig. Or it may be an 1,800-pound bull moose that at any time can run out and challenge your right of way, which usually results in two losses: for the moose, his life, and for the truck, a major repair job to the hood, grill, radiator, and sometimes a whole lot more. Even hitting a caribou has been known to result in several thousand dollars' worth in damage. I recall an incident where a trucker had hit a very large moose, resulting in a week or more of downtime along with a very large repair bill, with the radiator, fenders, and hood all being replaced. When all the repairs were finished and the rig ready to go back on the road, the driver decided to have a sign painted on the bug deflector of his new hood. It read, "Here Moosey Moosey," and on his first trip up the Parks Highway heading to Fairbanks, he hit another big bull. The damages were equal to or more than those of the first incident. I never saw an invitation on his bug reflector after that, and I can assure you he took a lot of good-natured ribbing over it.

Over the years when I operated in Alaska and the North, we had seven major accidents, and although there were no fatalities with our company, several serious injuries resulted from these occurrences and several hundred thousand dollars were paid for loss or damage to equipment and cleanup costs. We were very fortunate because there were several fatalities during this time with other companies operating here. So if you multiply this by other companies—none of them operated accident free—the costs are astronomical. We had one truck on the Richardson Highway that left the road and turned 360 degrees completely over from the time it left the road, soared into midair and landed in a pristine Alaska lake, fully loaded with turbine fuel. The driver was thrown out of the truck, and fortunately landed in the water, thereby saving his life. This ended up a costly wreck, between the loss of equipment, cleanup, and the fines for the spill of this equipment into these waters. We had another rig lose control on the Richardson Highway coming off Thompson Pass, going at a high rate of speed at the bottom of a hill. It was a total loss of equipment and load, and both drivers were seriously injured. Three more accidents were caused by extremely slick roads with partial loss of load but no serious driver injury. My son, Bruce, rolled a truck within the city limits of Anchorage, going around a curve on Jewel Lake Road, due to a front-end suspension failure, resulting in total loss of load and minor injuries to himself. We lost another truck on the lower Richardson Highway due to driver error, which resulted in loss of truck and trailer with minor injuries to the driver. Of course, we had several others leave the road which did not result in spills or loss of equipment. All in all we were very lucky not to have had any fatalities in these crashes, as there were many cases in which drivers were killed. The Haul Road has had a very poor record with fatal crashes; however, better maintenance and improved roads have greatly reduced the dangers of the early days. With the military operating in Alaska over the years, these kids come in here from the South 48 and they're not accustomed to or have any idea about what they're getting into with road conditions. I've seen quite a few fatalities recorded. It's a shame, but it does happen.

I recall one time a big military wrecker went toward Glennallen on the Glenn Highway, down the Hicks Creek hill. This military wrecker went straight off the end of that thing and killed both of the boys in it. Another one out of Palmer was going down into the hill headed toward Glennallen, down at the bottom of the hill. The soldier went in and jackknifed the semi and he was killed in that also. There's not much they can do about it as far as training them—they have to learn on the spot. It's a tough, tough deal for them. I was heading to Glennallen, dropping down into the same Hicks Creek hill, when a car passed me headed down the hill, and as he entered the turn I could see he started to slide sideways, just past where the military wrecker had left the road. When I got down to the corner his car was in two separate pieces about 30 feet apart. He had hit a snowplow with its blade angled, and this car was cut totally in half. It had hit just behind the driver, and the guy didn't have a scratch on him. It was absolutely amazing that he wasn't killed

Chapter 16
Alaska's North Slope

To most all of the world, the discovery of oil on the North Slope of Alaska was really big news, but to the Eskimos who had lived there for many years, it was old news, since they had long used it in lamps after getting it from places where it seeps up out of the ground. A teacher in the village of Wainwright found oil coming out of the ground in 1914,

Gene Rogge's big Kenworth.

and saw it running into a lake inland a short ways from the Arctic Ocean. This discovery prompted Standard Oil company to seek out claims in the surrounding area, which were invalidated by President Warren Harding in 1923, because he had set aside a large area as a reserve for the U.S. Navy, and prospecting and drilling were not allowed in this area. This same scenario had been played out prior to this in Wyoming and two areas of California, designated as naval petroleum reserves. Alaska had the option of claiming 104 million acres and chose this naval petroleum reserve and the large area around Prudhoe Bay, after becoming the 49th state. The state entered into leases with Richfield and Sinclair oil companies, the total acreage consisting of approximately 900,000 acres. Oil was discovered in huge amounts in 1966, when a rig at Prudhoe Bay hit the bonanza.

After working for Union Oil Company both driving and doing mechanic work in the shop for several years, I left and went to work for an old-time company in Alaska, Bayless and Roberts Trucking Company.

Another view of Gene Rogge's big Kenworth.

Both the Bayless and Roberts families were old-time Alaskans. They and their fathers before had been moving freight into the McCarthy and Forty-Mile country for years, starting with horses and wagons. After I had worked for Bayless and Roberts for quite some time, both driving and doing mechanic work in the shop, oil was discovered on the North Slope, and all these Alaska trucking companies were gearing up to get in on the big push to supply oil-drilling equipment and supplies for developing this massive discovery. Bayless and Roberts, like most other trucking companies, had gone out and invested in additional trucks and trailers and equipment to meet the upcoming demand for this huge material and equipment supply.

Oscar Nolls, Clyde Paustain, and I left Copper Center for Fairbanks to load modular housing units on our 45-foot flatbed trailers. We were the first three of Bayless and Roberts' trucks to be dispatched to travel up the ice road. We got our loads on, then traveled together up to Fox, where we met up with a convoy composed of about 40 rigs. Together we made our way up to Hess Creek Hill, just south of the Yukon River. The whole outfit came to a halt, since there were approximately 50 rigs ahead of us that were hung up due to four or five outfits that had spun out going up this hill. Finally, after a couple of hours of waiting, one of the guys unloaded a Cat off his lowboy and started up the hill to

A GNATS truck heading toward Prudhoe Bay.

try and untangle them. The Cat had gone up the hill about 200 yards when it turned sideways and slid all the way back down to the bottom, partly on the Cat trail and the last 50 yards or so out through the brush and trees, creating a whole new trail right before a wide-eyed bunch of drivers who were standing there. At which point he got off and said that as far as he was concerned, the road could stay blocked.

Another fellow got on the Cat and worked his way up the hill alongside the road with his blade down, knocking over trees and brush, which gave him traction, and in about 45 minutes he had the road open and we were on our way again to the North Slope. This first trip to the Slope was very interesting, for we learned a lot about the rough roads and blowing snow. The wind was awesome at times. I recall a modular unit sitting on its side after having been blown over, including the flatbed trailer it had been sitting on. Apparently, the tractor that had been pulling it broke down and had been hauled off, and that gave an indication of how high and how hard the wind blew up there. Along with this came a ton of snow when that wind blew.

We completed the trip to the North Slope and we dropped our loads off, and we came back. We left on our own, the three of us, with no support equipment or whatever, and by the grace of the good Lord we went on down toward Bettles. I was following Clyde and Oscar and we were all totally worn out. All of a sudden we saw Oscar's truck veer off the road and out onto the hard pack snow. It traveled for about a quarter of a mile. I was sitting there wondering what in the world he was doing when he finally ran into a large snowdrift and abruptly stopped. He sheepishly got out of the truck and looked in our direction, shaking his head. It seems that he had fallen to sleep in spite of the rough road and we shut down for several hours before taking off again. At that point it was quite a task getting his truck back out, but we finally got it out with chains and great effort and digging, and headed on down the road.

The rest of the trip was pretty mundane, no massive problems. We had several spots where snow had blown across the road and had to either wham into it a few times in the trucks or in some cases we had a Cat from northbound equipment clear it out for us. We made it back in and got home and rested up for about 24 hours.

On the next trip we were hauling heavy equipment, some outlandish and unique equipment, rebuilt tank retrievers that were used during World War II. They had retrofitted them and made them up for hauling these massive, big trailers and extra heavy loads in off-road conditions. They were set up to pull 40-foot trailers that were 12 feet wide, and these trailers were capable of pulling loads of 50 tons or more. We also had a brand-new Kenworth. It was specially rebuilt by Gene Rogge for off-road travel. This truck was twice the size of a conventional KW, with huge, oversized tires, and was set up to haul two large Cats, one on front and one on the pull trailer. The power unit was a V12 GMC engine equipped with automatic transmission. This truck was just huge. The convoy looked like something out of a truck driver's nightmare, and it almost turned out that way. The outfit was known as Gnats—Great Northern Alaska Transportation System. It was owned by Gene Rogge, Howard Bayless, Frank Chapados, Mark Moore, Leo Schlotfeldt, and

John Rowlett. We took off out of Fairbanks, headed north with these big rigs, and made it to Hess Creek Hill. Gene Rogge had a D8 Cat on the front of his truck and a 966 Cat loader on the rear trailer.

Gene had clawed part of the way up the hill. He got very close to the top and just couldn't go any farther. It seems that with the chains he had on all the wheels, they were not getting any traction in spite of the fact that this rig was equipped with a front-wheel drive besides the tandem rear end. The thing even had a heavy lug-traction- type tire on it but the chains buried themselves very neatly down into the bottoms of the grooves on the tires

A GNATS truck retuning to Fairbanks.

and didn't do any good at all, because it was almost ice instead of snow. It was very icy. He fought these conditions for an hour or more, and at that point he decided that the only thing to do to get going was to get the Cat off the lowboy that I was pulling, so they sent a driver back downhill to have the Cat unloaded and brought up to them. The problem now was that on this narrow, uphill trail the Cat had to be offloaded over the down-hill side of the trailer onto the snow, because if dropped off the rear of the trailer onto the ice it would immediately slide out of control. The trucks were parked 40 or 50 feet behind and it would smash up a truck. These Cats were not equipped with ice grousers, and on this ice it was absolutely ludicrous to even try to move them on the road.

They dropped the tie-down chains and upon starting to move the Cat, it immediately slid over in an awkward angle on the ice-covered bed of the trailer and ended up with one track on the ground and the other on the trailer bed. After another bit of maneuvering we finally got the Cat fully on the ground and after clawing a path up the hill using the brush and small trees beside the Cat trail, the Cat finally got up to the stalled rig and using chains, pulled it out another 40 or 50 feet to the top of the hill. But at that point they had to drop the pull trailer to do this; they just could not move it with the whole setup, so they blocked up the pull trailer and left it there.

The business end of a big Cat ready to dig.

Then they took the cable off the open winch that was mounted behind the cab back to the rear unit and hooked it to pull it to the top of the hill. After getting the truck ahead, they pulled the cable back down the hill and hooked it onto the trailer and started winching it toward them. It had gone about 15 or 20 feet when all of a sudden the winch cable came loose and stripped the entire cable off the drum. It had not been attached to the drum at the factory, and this was a brand-new rig. Down the hill the trailer went, backward, for about 200 or 300 feet, then off the road, finally turning upside down. We were fortunate it did, because if it had gone very much farther it would have hit a truck, and probably would have killed the driver of the truck. The 966 loader sustained approximately $30,000 worth of damage and came close to hitting two men also. They jumped out of the way as the tongue on the trailer swung by as it tipped over. One of them was Bill Rogge, Gene's son. All in all, it was pretty lucky that no one ended up getting killed. After this occurred, we took off, leaving the trailer and loader where they sat.

The next afternoon we got across the Yukon River ice bridge and had all kinds of problems. We finally shut down altogether and sat for several hours, and finally got all our problems fixed and took off for Bettles. After resting up and getting some more mechanical problems

Gene Rogge at the wheel of his big Kenworth.

fixed, we hooked up with possibly 80 more trucks, making a convoy of approximately 100 rigs. We headed up toward Bettles, and regrouped and rested up a bit there, then took off a few hours later headed to Anatuvik Pass and Prudhoe Bay.

We ran for several hours and one of the tank retrievers came down with a problem. The driver kept stopping; he said the clutch wasn't working, so anyway I got out of my rig. I had my tools, and had him go ahead with the rest of the convoy, and I stayed there until I figured the clutch adjustment was bad. I went ahead and took off the inspection plate on the clutch, and actually adjusted the clutch, and after getting this done in about an hour, got into it and lo and behold, it still didn't work. I thought, man, this guy's burned the clutch completely out on this rig. Anyway, I sat there for a while and one of the southbound outfits came by, and I asked one of the guys if he would get up in the cab and shove the clutch in while I was underneath it observing it. I crawled underneath there and he shoved down on the clutch. The clutch rod, about 7 or 8 feet long—really long, from the clutch pedal linkage going up to the clutch housing itself—was long and very light, about quarter-inch material, and it was actually pushing instead of

Great Northern Alaska Transportation's (GNAT) cook shack.

pulling in order to release the clutch. It was bending down and would not release the clutch.

I had a bunch of hose clamps, took a hacksaw, cut a small spruce tree down, and hose-clamped that spruce tree to the iron rod. It stiffened up the rod enough that if you shoved down on the clutch pedal, it released the clutch without bending, so lo and behold, I was off and running. I caught up to the other outfit about six hours later and before we got into Anatuvik Pass, a big wind came up and blew the road shut. We sat there for almost 80 hours with the wind blowing so hard that the only thing visible was the inside of the cab. I felt very fortunate to be driving the big tank retriever at the time, because it had lots of room inside and it even had an army cot available for use during this downtime, and it was very well used. I spent a lot of hours in it during this storm delay. There were no CB radios and therefore you had no communication with the other trucks. If you were lucky, you had some good reading material to while away the hours while waiting for this storm to blow itself out. In this particular situation, being in a rig with a sleeper, or as in my case an extra-large oversized cab, made things a lot more bearable, which I can attest to because after this particular storm delay I was involved in several more and in far less comfortable rigs.

This tank retriever had the engine sitting right in the middle of the cab and by raising a plywood cover over it, the engine was readily available. This allowed access to the exhaust manifold, which served as a

Tank retriever heading north.

wonderful source of heat to cook with. By putting cans of food onto the manifold or next to the turbo you soon had a can of hot soup or other choice delicacy to chow down. It was almost as good as being in a motor home. This was a far cry from the other guys sitting in their cramped cabs and making do with cold sandwiches or whatever.

During these extreme conditions, it is virtually impossible to leave the confines of the truck cab, and after several hours or less of sitting there, you started to become inclined to relieve yourself. This can suddenly become a challenge, depending on whether it's number 1 or number 2. A gallon can or jar can take care of number 1; however, number 2 is another story. I can only talk for myself as I'm certain we each had our own method of getting the job done. I personally carried along the trusty Folgers coffee can for number 2, and carried a large roll of aluminum foil, which formed a very nice receptacle that could be neatly folded together after the fact and disposed of at a later time. I carried mine in a garbage bag and disposed of them in the proper fashion. However, I'm not convinced that the many little aluminum foil packages I saw lying in various spots along the trail contained leftover parts of sandwiches that drivers had tossed out of their windows. And for certain, I was not curious enough to unwrap any of them to find out. I often wondered what took place in situations like the above, when three or four drivers were huddled up together in one truck, and the wind blowing 100 miles an hour outside?

When this storm finally died down, we were in a real mess. Some of the

rigs were buried in drifts of snow and after several hours we finally got dug out and were underway. It was quite a chore. Several miles up the trail, we came across 10 or 12 rigs that belonged to Pioneer Alaska Express, owned by Wayne King. That the storm was over didn't mean that the wind had died—it was still blowing profusely, but not

Great Northern Alaska Transportation's (GNAT) logo.

enough to shut us down, when we came upon these rigs. They had gotten blown in by the same storm and these drivers realized that if they continued to sit there all the trucks would run out of fuel, and if the storm continued they could be endangering their lives. So they managed to siphon fuel out of the shut-down rigs and refuel the ones left running, and then they piled into the three or four trucks left running. None of these trucks had sleepers on them; they were just conventional cabs, and with three or four big truck drivers with gear on, you got a very compact arrangement in the cab. We had never seen a more tired or disheveled bunch of drivers than these fellows were. We went to work with our equipment and dug out these trucks and trailers, fueled them up, and after three or four hours were finally underway again. These guys were very grateful to have gotten some good food under their belts and to get cleaned up, and they were ready to go on the road. Some of these outfits had Cats with them and some didn't. In this case, these guys did not have a Cat; they were hauling other equipment. Since they had no road-clearing equipment, they were relying on other convoys coming along, and we happened to be the first.

On the way north, we stopped at Anatuvik Pass, and notified the state road crew that one rig, Gene Rogge's truck and trailer, would be coming back through early that afternoon to go back south with them, because all the outfits had been notified that when our convoy went through the pass, the state was pulling everything back south. We were the very last

Cliff Bishop and crippled tank retriever.

ones headed to Prudhoe for the year. We then proceeded to Anatuvik Pass, to an inland Eskimo settlement. I had, at this time, made five or six trips; this was one of the last of the season, and Charley Barr had brought Gene Rogge's old yellow Kenworth tanker, truck, and trailer to supply fuel for our convoy. I had all I wanted of the ice road at this time and volunteered to drive this rig back to Fairbanks by myself. I was thinking that I could get back several days ahead of the guys going to Prudhoe Bay, and Charley, being the nice guy that he is, agreed.

We traded rigs. After fueling up all the equipment that was going north to Prudhoe, I started filling 55-gallon drums to leave with the Eskimos with the balance of the fuel as the last of the convoy went up out of sight, headed on up through this huge valley. It took me about two hours to get this done, and within this time what had been gentle breezes blowing on a very calm afternoon, became increasingly hard winds, and I knew I had to hurry to get back to the trail south in order to meet up with the state road crew. I topped my own fuel tanks off and made certain that I left 200 or 300 gallons in the tanker, and headed back south through Anatuvik Pass. I'd been back on the trail for only a short while and started getting snowdrifts blown onto the trail by a wind that obviously was increasing as my visibility was decreasing. And the drifts were rapidly getting deeper. I was wishing I could turn around and go back to the village; however, with 4- or 5-foot and deeper shoulders the Cats had dozed up, turning around was not an option. I started hitting drifts that required me to stop and back up a few feet to ram on through them. With this,

Cliff Bishop in control of the oversized tank retriever.

and the rapidly decreasing visibility, I started realizing that I wasn't going to go much farther. I also realized that when I stopped I was going to be there until the storm was over and probably quite a while longer, since my truck was the last one headed south.

I didn't make it very much farther when I hit a drift that brought me to a complete stop. While sitting there for two or thee hours I began to realize that maybe this shortcut back to Fairbanks with all its amenities, hot food, warm bath, a nice soft bed, and so on, just maybe would have worked out better if I'd continued north with the rest of the gang.

I found out later that the State had left a couple of pieces of equipment in the pass for several hours waiting after the main group headed back to Bettles, and after waiting several hours and the weather turning bad, they decided that we had changed our minds and had headed back to Prudhoe with all the equipment.

Well, the longer I sat there the worse the wind got, and with temperatures dropping from 5 or 10 degrees above zero as they had been

Cliff Bishop repairing springs on oversize Kenworth.

Gene Rogee and his big rig.

A road side repair job on tire chains.

A younger Cliff Bishop.

Bill Rogee.

all day, to minus 15 degrees in a matter of three or four hours, I knew that I was in for a nasty spell. I was sitting there thinking that at least I had shelter within this old Kenworth even if it was crowded and as long as the engine kept running I'd be OK. I glanced down at my feet and where the clutch pedal comes up through the floorboards there was a pile of snow almost up to the top of the clutch itself, very neatly rising like a pyramid, being forced in around the rubber grommet on the pedal by this huge wind. I watched in fascination as this pile was getting

My old friend, Gene Rogge getting water at Anatuvik Pass.

bigger and the thought occurred to me that if this continued I could possibly be completely covered in a few more hours. Enough of those thoughts—I took a rag and stuffed it around the pedal, and put an efficient stop to this imagined danger.

In the first part of the storm, I got out and took the air hose off the air cleaner outside, which is mounted on the outside of the cab, and put the suction end back under the hood, next to the engine and fire walls, to keep a supply of air to the engine. If left hooked up to the outside, there was a good chance that the air cleaner would clog up with blowing snow and kill the engine. With this chore accomplished, I had nothing more to do other than sit there for what seemed like an eternity listening to that old Cummins engine running at a fast idle.

With no sleeper on the old tanker and with extra clothes and emergency rations stacked up on the passenger side of the cab, I had very little room to move around, and pretty much the steering wheel became my pillow for the next 80 or so hours. After what seemed like an eternity, I awoke with a start and realized that there was a shudder in the steering wheel and a definite roughness in the engine that I couldn't hear as much as feel, and realized that the engine had a definite miss in it. I immediately increased the hand throttle to increase the rpm, which had the effect of smoothing out the roughness.

I knew almost immediately that the probable cause was a clogged fuel filter. That was a common problem we ran into, and I knew that it could possibly get much worse and even cause the engine to shut down entirely. With the wind blowing as it was, getting out and changing it would be a near-impossible task. It was blowing hard enough that it

To Alaska's North Slope.

was actually shaking the cab. I also realized that if the engine did shut down, this predicament would become a life-or-death situation in a matter of hours. I had not paid any attention to how long I had been there until this engine issue came up, at which time I tried to estimate just how long it was, and to the best of my guessing it was about 35 to 40 hours. After having been tied up several times for periods of 15 or 20 hours, and periods of more than 80 hours in prior storms, I could only hope that this would soon blow over.

I sat there by the hour with this rough-running engine, trying to stay awake, and would drift off into a half sleep and then come fully awake and realize that the engine was still running. I couldn't keep my eyes open any longer and lay over the steering wheel, and how long I slept I have no idea. I was absolutely beat.

Suddenly, from the other side of the truck, I heard a loud noise, a hammering noise. I jumped over on top of the stuff in the passenger seat, rolled the window down and looked out, and there was an Eskimo in a parka standing on an old snowmachine next to the truck. I noticed that the sun was shining and there was no wind blowing whatsoever. I had obviously been sound asleep.

When this rescuer arrived with a big smile on his face, and asked me if I would like to go to the village with him, I reached down and shut the engine off, gathered up a small bunch of clothing and gear, and

A common sight on the haul road.

after putting on my parka I got on the back of his old snowmachine and we headed back 6 or 7 miles to the village. I don't know whether they heard the truck running or this man had just been out running around, but in any event I was just happy to see him. His name was Jack Ahgook, and we went back to his place in the village.

This village is the farthest inland village occupied by Eskimos in Alaska, and possibly in Canada also. The reason they were so far inland is that their main food supply was the massive caribou herd that migrates through every year. In years past, they had made a long trip from the coast inland to get meat, and to haul it out again. Ultimately, they made this area their full-time home. They were also unique in the fact that the typical Eskimo diet is derived from the ocean, from seal, whale, fish, and other aquatic creatures. This village had a diet which offered very little, if any fish.

Jack's home was situated on ground level and had a dugout-type lower level, which constituted the main living quarters. In addition to Jack and his wife, there were two little kids and an older daughter. I was welcomed into their home and treated like visiting royalty. In the next few days I was taken to most of the other families' places and heard many stories about their hunting exploits with caribou, and their methods of keeping meat stored in underground dugouts for long periods of time. I had several meals prepared from the caribou that had been taken way back before winter set in, and it was absolutely delicious. I recall watching the kids play in a tub of water, and floating some little items in it. When the coffee was made, guess where the water came from? It still

A cold day at Anatuvik Pass.

tasted really good, and I'll always remember Jack's friendly smile when he picked me up, and the novelty of living the Eskimo lifestyle. I only wish their home had been an igloo instead.

There were some airplane flights which brought in needed supplies, so the village wasn't totally isolated, and I planned to fly out on the next flight that came in, knowing that my truck was going to be stuck there for a long time to come. At the time I shut the engine off, the thought occurred to me that it might be a really long time before that old Kenworth would be rescued, if ever.

About four days after I moved in with Jack Ahgook and his family, I observed four or five rigs headed down the valley toward Anatuvik Pass. Because of the high cost of flying their rigs on the Hercules airplanes, the truckers decided to fight their way back on the abandoned Haul Road from Prudhoe Bay back to Fairbanks, hoping to catch up with the state crew before it left. But they had been held up also, and we were all stuck in that respect.

When I told them of my predicament, they said, "Well, let's go. We'll help you get out." I got into one of the trucks and we made our way down to where my snow-covered rig was sitting, and after a lot of shoveling, putting on a new fuel filter, and fire-potting the engine, we got everything underway and headed south, with my truck leading the way. These rigs had made their way back thus far by using the front truck as a battering ram, and would come as hard as they could at the snowdrifts, hook two or three trucks on a cable, and pull the lead truck back before going at it again, and going on to the next drift.

Once my truck was running again, we hooked chains on it, pulled it

Rough road

backward for a short ways and broke it loose from the built-up snow, and after clearing a path with our shovels we got underway heading south, with my truck in the lead. I charged ahead with my truck and ran into the snowdrifts as hard as I could, after which they pulled me back with the chains, and did it again. We also used our shovels. Part of this trip we got a break by traveling down a windblown river for a long way before getting back on the ice road. What was unique about this river was that you could look down through the ice and see gravel, probably 5 or 6 feet below, and yet clear as a bell. At long last we made it back to Bettles. These hardworking Montana truckers decided to lay over in Bettles for a couple of days and rest up. I decided that I was not going to stop and I continued down the trail.

My decision to head to Fairbanks on my own came from the fact that traffic had gone down not too far ahead of me, and I anticipated few bad spots. There were several drifts, but since I could see most of these from a long way off, I would speed up fast as I could go to hit them, and I made it through some drifts that one would not generally make it through. But by sheer speed and power, I made it through without getting stopped. The guys I left behind, the Montana guys, waited about 24 hours after my departure to get back on the road, and they had hell coming down. Another big blow came through, and again they fought their way back.

They were a week behind me coming into Fairbanks; one of their trucks even ran off the road and turned over. By going, I avoided all of this. I finally made it back into Fairbanks, totally worn out.

On each of these trips into the Arctic, there were many and varied experiences. The majority of the drivers had never been exposed to these harsh conditions, most of them coming up from the South 48, since the driver base in Alaska didn't come close to supplying enough extra drivers for this massive undertaking. The drivers who were in Alaska were 95% full-time employees to start with. It was quite a sight to see 60 or more trucks in these convoys going up steep hills and across snow-blown tundra and ice-covered lakes. You have to give a lot of credit to the drivers who came to Alaska in 1969 and again in 1973 and were involved in the transportation of equipment to the North Slope on the Hickel Highway and then on the Dalton Highway and the Haul Road.

The vast majority of these drivers had never operated on snow-covered roads and certainly had never seen temperatures in the subzeros ranging down to as much as 70 below. Operating on snow- and ice-covered roads

Winter arctic sky.

was indeed a test of their will and determination to get the job done and in spite of their lack of experience, they rose to the challenge and succeeded under these harsh conditions. It was a common sight to see trucks and trailers covered with ice and snow sitting along the trail, broken down. If a rig had problems, they would just leave it there and go on with the convoy and pick it up on the return trip south. Almost never did any of these broken-down rigs get repaired out there on the spot, since it was just not possible under these conditions. I was able to keep several of our trucks going because I carried a large supply of backup parts and plenty of tools, and was used to working under adverse conditions, so unless it was a major breakdown such as an engine, transmission, or rear end, I was usually able to fix the problem.

I recall one incident that anywhere else except where we were would have been considered at best just a minor repair. This was a heater motor that quit and the driver could not keep going. Not so much because of the cold, but because the windshield fogged up so much that he couldn't see out. So he stopped and the whole convoy shut down behind him. I went back to his truck and after finding out what his problem was, I went back to my rig, got some tools, and removed the heater motor. As I suspected, the brushes had worn completely out and were no longer making contact on the armature. The motor totally quit. This truck had only one single heater in it. It was imperative that we get this motor going or abandon the truck and his load, and these were high-dollar loads, $12,000 to $13,000 loads. I started thinking about this for a few minutes, and the closest parts store being 200 or 300 miles away, had to come up with an answer. I suddenly remembered reading in an article in *Popular Mechanics* years before that a person needing a piece of carbon for whatever reason had taken a D flashlight battery and cut it open.

YUKON • RIVER
ICE MAY BE UNSAFE
CROSS AT YOUR
OWN • RISK
STATE OF ALASKA DEPT. OF HIGHWAYS

A fair warning from the state.

Inside was a carbon core. So, never having done this, I found one of the trucks that had a flashlight with D batteries in it and proceeded to cut one of them open. Sure enough, there was my carbon. I took a knife and fashioned a square piece to fit into the brush holder; using the small piece left from the original brush with the wire still attached, I put the new carbon in and then set what was left of the original brush on top of it, and with the hold-down spring placed on top, I put it back together. Lo and behold, it worked. So in a short while, we were off and running again, and made our deliveries. This brush that I made lasted until the truck got back to Fox, north of Fairbanks, at which point it finally gave up. The driver continued into Fairbanks because it was just a short ways left to go, and he got it repaired there. The carbon in the battery was obviously made of a much lighter material than they use in regular brushes, so it wore down really fast, but it got the job done and we got the thing back on the road again.

We finished our last trip after many long hours of fighting rough

Cliff Bishop cutting off the end of the truck frame, It was contacting the bottom of the trailer when going over tops of hills and stopping the truck.

North Slope Ice Road and wind blowing snow.

(right) Gene Rogee on top of load on his oversize Kenworth.

(below) Gene Rogee and his son, Bill Rogee, with his back to the camera.

(below right) Cliff Bishop tightening lug nuts.

A Bishop Trucking tanker along the haul road.

terrain, bitter cold temperatures, sleepless nights, and endless hours of driving from Fairbanks to the North Slope. I got back into Glennallen, where I was living at the time, and stepped on the scale after taking a bath, and discovered that I had lost 22 pounds from the time I had started out a few weeks earlier. I had never missed a meal, and had never been sick. It was purely from exhaustion and many, many hours of not sleeping.

Chapter Seventeen
Northern Lights

One of the most awesome sights of these trips and within the Arctic Circle was the northern lights. And though I had seen them for many years, from Fairbanks and south of Anchorage, and even on the Kenai Peninsula, it was so much more spectacular and colorful within the Arctic Circle. At times they seemed to reach clear to the ground, and though I've seen them numerous times I would come to a complete stop if I was in a position to do so and not hold up trucks behind me. Occasionally when this happened I just sat there and admired these beautiful displays. I had never seen these lights come down so close to the ground. In Fairbanks and Anchorage they were most always high in the sky, but here within the Arctic Circle, with the snow in all directions, and on occasion with the moon shining, the display of lights made it seem almost like you were on another planet. There was something special about these northern lights that was almost spellbinding, and I have heard people say that they actually could hear a certain noise or sound as they flashed overhead. I personally can't say I have ever heard this, but I tend to believe that it is true, and many swear to it.

CHAPTER 18
Environmental Challenge

After this winter of 1969, fighting the elements and succeeding, hauling to Prudhoe Bay many tons of equipment and other supplies necessary to start the drilling to put this massive discovery into production, with huge numbers of Cats, front-end loaders, oil-drilling equipment, and trucks, there was a challenge by environmentalists that put a complete halt to trucking, and the pipeline project went on hold for a period of four years. This action was an absolute disaster to the trucking and construction companies that had invested millions of dollars to prepare for this big boom. They had geared up in order to provide support services such as trucking pipe and all equipment and supplies that would be required to put this multimillion-dollar project into production. With the delay created by the environmental block, construction costs soared. The equipment sat idle for all that time with payments or at least interest payments having to be made. In some cases an awful lot of repossessions took place, as well as bankruptcies. In addition, the overall cost of the project escalated by many millions of dollars, which most certainly was passed on and increased the prices of fuel. The government, by an act of Congress in 1973, put all challenges to this project to rest.

Chapter Nineteen
Building the Haul Road

The oil companies immediately started developing the North Slope. They put a huge hovercraft on the Yukon River that was capable of hauling four loaded trucks across the river on each trip, and started building the Haul Road in early 1974, completing it in November 1974. A bridge over the Yukon was completed in 1975. This did away with the hovercraft and the use of ice crossings. The pipeline was finally started in 1974, and took four years to complete. A bridge was built across the Yukon River in 1975, replacing the ice bridge that had been used in winter months and replacing the huge hovercraft that was used during the summer months. With the completion of the Yukon River bridge, the truckers were required to stop at a guard station and present an Alyeska pass. The truckers were also charged $1.07 per mile for use of the Haul Road to help with maintenance costs. This arrangement lasted from 1974 to 1977, when it became a public road.

The Haul Road has been vastly improved over the years from when it first opened to travel, and though greatly improved, remains one of the most difficult roads to be tackled by truckers anywhere. The road has claimed many lives since opening in 1974. At any given time, there can be 100 trucks or more on this road to the Arctic Ocean, and at times visibility is virtually nonexistent, forcing rigs to come to a complete standstill. You can only hope that someone doesn't come along and slam into you while you are stopped, or worse, that you travel on your side of the road under these conditions and find another rig appearing smack dab in the middle coming at you, a scenario that unfortunately for some was the last thing they ever saw. Although statistics have proved beyond doubt that this road is no place for beginners, many drivers have traveled the route for many years, some accounting for over a million miles on it, and one thing is certain: there are a lot of miles between coffee stops on this road. After leaving the Hilltop truck stop just north of Fairbanks on the Elliott Highway, it is a distance of 414 miles to Deadhorse on the Dalton Highway, with only one place in between to get a cup of coffee and a sandwich at mile 175 on the Dalton. This is the farthest-north truck stop in the world, Coldfoot Services. The trip from Fairbanks to Prudhoe Bay is usually done in approximately 13 to 14 hours in decent weather conditions, but can last for an awful lot longer if you get caught up in some of the storms that this part of Alaska can present you from time to time. Temperatures to 70 below zero and hurricane-force winds with drifting snow at other times make these trips last much longer. Also, the size and weight of the loads vary from an average 30 to 40 tons. Drilling modules weighing up to 200,000 pounds or more require extra push trucks to work in tandem with the lead tractor to get these massive loads up the hills and to their destinations. Grades range from 14% and up. These grades are quite a challenge when covered with ice and snow. Atigun Pass is close to 5,000 feet in altitude in the Brooks Range and has been blessed with many avalanches over the years. However, since the State began using a cannon to blast the slide areas, the road has become much safer for truckers. This trip remains a challenge to any and all who tackle it, regardless of how many times they have been up and down the road in the past. You can get caught up in one of the massive storms that are known to hit this area at any given time and that can shut you down, at which time you are thankful that the extra emergency rations were not forgotten, because it could be several hours before you get underway again. The other thing you are thankful for is that big arctic-grade sleeping bag in the sleeper. In trucking this road in the winter months, you don't have to go very far without seeing the telltale marks of where some unfortunate driver hit the ditch and left an off-road signature for all to see. The Dalton Highway with its steep grades requires a driver to use a lot of speed on the downhill slopes in order to get over the top of the next snow-covered hill without spinning out, and this fast approach also accounts for some of the ditch-diving rigs when things get out of control. Experienced drivers will use speeds up to 70 or so miles per hour in order to be assured of getting over the top of the next hill without spinning out, and avoid the possibility of sliding backward and possibly off the road.

The challenges for loads going over the haul road change dramatically when truckers are required to transport huge, 200,000 plus loads. These loads require the use of push trucks with rubber pads mounted on their front bumpers. Others used a large steel shaft connecting the push truck to the load being assisted. Push truck rigs assist in getting over the many hills that exceed 14 percent grade slopes. At times, depending on road conditions and load weight, it is necessary to use three or more push trucks to get these load to their destination. The drivers on push truck are almost driving blind with the only sense of direction being the rig in front of them. They are unable to see the road because the truck they're pushing blocks their view. At times, due to blowing snow or dust they even lose sight of the rig they are pushing. When this happens they need to stay pushing tight against the lead truck or else risk losing the road altogether.

When on an upgrade slope, if the push truck backs off it is possible that the whole outfit will come to a complete stop. Getting started again can be a real problem, which if not done properly could result in broken drive lines and other parts. Drivers of these trucks are experienced and the loads usually proceed and reach their destinations without undo problems.

Another use of push trucks is in descending steep grades. The push truck will proceed around in front of the lead truck and assist in braking by putting his front bumper against the lead truck. This makes a much safer descent. It is not uncommon for all the push trucks and the lead truck to be chained up on all axles.

For weight on a bob-tail push truck a 34,000 pound block is attached to the 5th wheel and bolted to the tie downs on the tractor. In many cases push trucks are also carrying loaded trailers with enough weight for good pushing traction. If necessary, the 34,000 pound block is also mounted on the nose of the trailer. This whole operation is a sight to behold when under operation.

There were a lot of deaths on this road over the years and it wasn't always the new, inexperienced drivers; some of the older, seasoned drivers also were involved, for this road was a true challenge to all who traveled it. Sam Little, a longtime Alaskan and Alcan trucker, wrote a song about it called "The Kamikaze Trail." The song very well illustrates the dangers of this road. The drivers usually carry emergency supplies such as extra hose clamps, filters, a small bag of tools, and a good supply of emergency food rations. Of course, these things are a good idea to carry anywhere you travel in the north country.

Chapter Twenty
Start of Bulk Plant

I stayed with Bayless and Roberts a couple of years longer and on my day off I made a trip into Anchorage and stopped by the Union Oil bulk plant in Palmer to visit with Walt Briggs. He also owned the plant in Glennallen. He asked if I would be interested in buying it and I told him I would buy the state of Alaska if the terms were right. We did a handshake agreement and agreed on a price of $375,000.

I went back to Glennallen and contacted Howard Bayless and told him of my plans. He gave me a handshake and wished me luck on this new venture. I began racking my brain as to how I was going to come up with the money to make this happen. Walt wanted $25,000 down, and at that particular time I probably had a total of $25 to my name. I had a couple of old houses there in Glennallen that I had bought from the State, and I contacted my nephew, Sam Bishop, who agreed to buy one of them for about $12,000, which left me only $13,000 short. In those days we had a bank in Glennallen located in a mobile home. I went into Palmer a few days later and gave Walt a check for $25,000. I knew it took at least a week for it to get back to my bank in those days. Nonetheless, we were still short by approximately half of the amount. In any event, we took over the operation and went to work hauling fuel. We had what are called sight drafts, meaning that when we hauled a load of fuel for the bulk plant we could immediately write a check to ourselves to pay for the freight charges, since we operated the trucking as a common carrier and the bulk plant as a Union Oil consignee, and we received a commission for the product that was sold through the plant. I went to the banker and told him what I had done and asked him to call me the minute the check from Walt showed up. At this point the banker said, "You didn't have to do this. I would let you have a loan in that amount to get started." The check showed up in about ten days from the time I gave it to Walt, since in those days all bank transactions were done by mail, and in the meantime I had hauled enough loads that along with the day-to-day sales it more than covered the outstanding check.

We started this operation as commission agents and in less than a year we took over as jobbers, which meant that we purchased the product directly from Union Oil and then sold it to the public, making a much better deal for us and certainly more profitable. After making this initial down payment all that was left to do was pay out another $350,000 to pay off the debt. I figured it would take a lifetime to do this. We went to work and put as many hours in as was possible every day and were fortunate to get some good fueling contracts for different road projects and also several State contracts for schools and State road camps throughout the Interior.

By this time all of the equipment had been sitting on the North Slope for about three years because of the environmental challenges and we didn't know when or if this project would ever get off the ground, but lo and behold, it did happen. The Alyeska people came to us and asked for a supply of fuel to start the pipeline construction with, so we went to work hauling small amounts of fuel to various worksites. This soon developed into a massive contract; the fact is we were running eight of our own trucks and hired 10 more and ran 24 hours per day until the construction phase was completed. By the end of the construction we had paid off the bulk plant and after another year or so we sold out and took a well-earned vacation after working for four years, seven days a week, and not having time to enjoy being in the Alaska outdoors.

Chapter Twenty-One
Mining

I had always wanted to try my hand at gold-mining, long before coming north, after hearing all the stories my grandfather, Howard Bishop, told of his trips to the Yukon. I've always held the opinion that the only way to enjoy Alaska is to retire and move outside and then return here as a tourist, because while living and working here it seems you never find time to do these fun things. In any event, I got my two sons, Clifford and Bruce, along with a friend, Bob Ellis, and we outfitted a gold-mining expedition into the Wrangell Range near McCarthy. I had a bush pilot friend, Steph Strunk, who did all our air transport from Copper Center into the Bremner area, and after numerous trips, we had gotten the 6-inch dredge, diving suit, and all the food, gas, and other supplies in place, and we all flew in. The plane left us there to pursue our buried fortunes. We had done a lot of research on this area and the old-timers had taken several million dollars in gold out of this area back in the old days. Most of this was done by tunneling under the mountains using a stamp mill to remove the gold from the hard rock. Our theory was that they had worked the platforms above the river-bed and that the river itself had never been mined. We had the dredge disassembled and had to carry it in pieces from the bush landing strip to the creek, and put it back together. We finally got everything operational and after two days of dredging we came up with one very small nugget. Not to be discouraged, we packed up and moved another mile downstream and started again. This sounds easy; however, it requires a whole lot of hard work to move this very heavy dredge and all the support equipment along with it. After my very first dive and less than an hour's work we had several nice nuggets. We were very glad to actually see these beautiful nuggets, and were a very happy bunch of miners. After another seven or eight days we accumulated enough gold to pay for our investment. We had made a prior arrangement to have the plane come and check on us on the 12th day. By that time we were kind of running out of enthusiasm, groceries, and gas.

We decided to stash our equipment and come back later, because we were getting into good pay ground and on the day the plane was supposed to arrive and check on us the decision was made for me to wait at the airstrip with some of the things we were going to take back out. The others were going down to where the dredge was located to secure it and carry out gas cans and other items.

I'd been sitting at the airstrip for about three or four hours waiting for the plane to show up and began to wonder if I had miscalculated the days and was there on the wrong day, because there were no signs of the plane showing up. What I didn't know at the time was that although the weather was beautiful where we were, the plane was located at the Birchwood airport near Anchorage. The high winds had kept the plane from taking off and it actually didn't get there until the next day. I was sitting there about half asleep and looked across the canyon and saw a huge grizzly bear with a cub. Having my movie camera with me, I decided to take some footage of them. After I'd been filming for several minutes they disappeared down toward the creek bottom, and out of my sight. And after waiting there a bit I decided to walk over to the canyon edge and try and get some more footage of them as they went down the streambed.

I turned the camera on as I got within a few feet of the edge, ready to capture more of this Alaska wildlife, and as I looked over the edge and down toward the creek bottom I was greeted by this huge grizzly running straight up the hill toward me. Had she been walking instead of taking big leaps toward me, I don't think it could have bothered me as much. My reaction to this sight was an abrupt 180. I turned and ran 75 or 80 feet across the airstrip to where there were three empty 55-gallon gas drums. I ducked down behind one of them and as I looked between the two barrels about 50 feet away, coming straight toward me in all her glory was this furry creature with the big teeth and claws. I thought, Oh hell, what a way to go! I reached down beside me and picked up a large rock. I guess I picked it up and thought it was something to protect myself with. Anyway, as I peeked around the edge of the barrel, I was no longer able to see her between the barrels—she was still coming directly toward me and less than 25 feet away. I suspect she smelled the lunch meat and other food items I had with me. In any event, I had to do something other than try to hit her, which would only have made her mad, so I hit the empty barrel as hard as I could with the rock and made a pretty loud sound. At that point, she stood straight up on her hind legs and I could see her over the top of the barrel. She dropped straight back down so I hit the barrel again, and looking out between the barrels again I saw the cub running away from me, 25 or 30 feet away, and in just a couple of seconds the sow disappeared, heading toward the cub.

I can't say for certain, but I think the second time I hit the barrel it scared the cub, and when it ran its mother followed. The tail end of that bear was the most beautiful sight I had ever seen. I don't know if I handled this situation correctly or not—I've had different opinions expressed to me by various people over the years. The only thing I know for certain is that in retrospect, it must have been correct. Because I came away from this encounter in one piece and also with documented proof that I am a coward, for I left the camera running after I turned it on by the edge of the bank. All you can see of my dash across the airstrip is my feet being photographed as I'm retreating toward the barrels, one following the other in a very rapid fashion. This whole scenario was totally against what I had often stated, that I wouldn't be caught 50 feet off any road in Alaska without having my rifle with me. We had only one gun with us, and the boys took it because I was only supposed to be there for a little bit waiting for the airplane. I will tell you this much—never again was I caught without a gun. I brought my own rifle back with me and I kept it with me from there on out. A gun in your hand gives you a lot better feeling of security than a rock.

In any event, I came back for another 10 days and then we all left to take a break for a few days, and get more supplies. We had wanted to come back and make another trip before the snow flew, but my nephew Sam Bishop and Larry Bowen had filed a legal claim about 300 yards downstream from where we were prospecting, and they had hired a helicopter to fly their dismantled backhoe and their equipment into the claim. They had set up a mining operation for about two weeks when they were visited by a helicopter full of national park rangers. The rangers informed them that the claims were no longer valid, because this whole area was now located within the newly created Wrangell Saint Elias National Park, and to cease and desist their mining operation or face prosecution.

There went our hopes for golden riches. When they got out they called and told us of these new developments. What we were able to pick up from our prospecting, and the gold that Sam and Larry were just getting into when they were shut down indicated to me that the stretch of gravel bar in the stream below holds a wealth of gold. With the whole area being shut down, we left our dredge and our equipment until the following year when we returned and hauled everything out. I still daydream about the bonanza that would have resulted in a fortune if worked with the proper equipment. Jimmy Carter through this designation made this a national park, making certain that no one will ever touch this particular area or the tens of thousands of acres surrounding it. The rules after they made this a national park forbade the use of any motorized equipment. We were told that it was permissible to take a gold pan, but a shovel was not allowed. So even recreational mining is effectively forbidden. The area we were in lay downstream from where the old-timers did their mining and the records verify that millions of dollars were recovered before this area was abandoned and the downstream area where we were had never been touched. The mining had been effectively curtailed.

Because the railroad into the McCarthy area had been shut down and abandoned many years before, there was no effective transportation system to keep this mining area operational, gold being of only very low value in those days, somewhere around $15 an ounce or less compared to the $700 an ounce or more that it is today.

Chapter Twenty-Two
Hunting Alaska

I think that most everyone who moves to Alaska has an interest in the great outdoors, hunting and fishing and so forth, and if they don't have the interest upon arriving here, they certainly acquire it afterward. I recall my first hunting trip for moose. Back in those days we used to wait for the late hunting season when we could use snowmachines and cross over the frozen lakes and get up into the high country. On my first trip, we went out on the last day of the season, out of Tanada Lake up in the Nabesna country. We took off at about six o'clock in the morning and headed up into the Wrangell Mountains. It was extremely cold, 64 degrees below zero at Tanada Lake, when we left the lodge there. Dick Fredricks had a lodge near Tanada Lake called Sportsman's Paradise Lodge. Jim Johnson, Dick's son Doug Fredricks, and I took off from there on three snowmachines, pulling sleds behind each of them. We got up to Copper Lake to an old cabin there. It had no doors or windows but did have an old stove, and as we got into the higher elevations there was an extreme temperature change. I recall a thermometer on the side of this cabin and the temperature range on this thermometer was from 120 degrees above to 80 degrees below zero. It was so cold that all of the mercury in the thermometer was in the little round bulb at the bottom of the glass. The temperature was lower than minus 80 degrees. We went in and finally got a little fire started in the stove. There was some scrap wood there. We had to use some gasoline mixed with oil that we were carrying on the snowmachines. We poured this on the wood and I recall throwing a match on this gas, which would normally light up in a hurry, but the match sat on it and flickered like a candle. It finally did take off, and we got a fire going after a while and warmed up somewhat. We were probably 45 minutes to an hour getting all this done.

We went out and started the snowmachines up, ready to go up to the hunting area, and the snowmachines wouldn't go. It was so cold that the tracks had frozen in place. We got them running by tipping them over on their sides with one guy revving the engine up full throttle and the other guy kicking on the track. Finally it got going around and around. We did this on all three machines and took off up the hill and sure enough, we ran into a little herd of moose. A nice big bull came trotting out. I leveled on him, except the gun wouldn't go off. It was so cold that the firing pin would not strike the bullet hard enough to fire the shell. I kept digging in my pockets and refilling the gun, and after emptying the unfired shells and putting more in, kept pulling the trigger hoping that a bullet would fire. Finally, after the bull was about gone over the hill a couple of hundred yards away, the gun finally did shoot, and I killed the moose. I think there were something like 15 bullets lying on the ground that I had levered out but had not fired. Our work was cut out for us at that point.

Doug butchered the moose with our help, very little that it was. Doug did most of it. We got it cut up and loaded on the sleds. We took off back to Tanada Lake; it was very slow going and an extremely cold trip. We got back at about seven or eight o'clock that evening, I've never been so tired and so completely worn out, as were the other guys—actually a rather foolish situation, one that I would never attempt again in that kind of temperature. It was absolutely the coldest I have ever been, and everything we did reflected it, from the gun not firing to coming back in the dark. It just absolutely kicked our butts before it was over and done with, but we got'er done, and got our moose.

Hank Osborn, an old-time friend, and I were on another hunting trip on our snowmachines in the same area a year or two after this first moose trip. We went out across Tanada Lake and the wind was blowing very, very strongly. I had a large sled behind me with a snowmachine pulling it loaded with supplies. We were going to spend two or three days in a cabin Dick and Doug had just built at Copper Lake. They had built it after we'd been there on our first trip. We were going across the lake in a big, wide-open, wind-swept area The wind was blowing extremely hard and I was progressing across the lake ahead of Hank when all of a sudden my snowmachine started sliding sideways. The trailer decided to handle just like a truck would, like a semi jackknifing. The wind had caught me and blew the whole outfit probably 50 feet off the line of direction I was moving in. The lake in this area was absolutely blown clean. The outfit hit an ice ridge going sideways—this ridge sat up about 4 or 5 inches, and it turned the whole outfit over

Cliff Bishop's son, Bruce, age 13, with a moose he and his dad took in the Wrangell Mountains.

and threw me off. I had a gun strapped on my back and when I landed I landed on my side and then rolled over on my back. I hit so hard that it broke the stock on the gun. All the supplies went off the trailer and scattered, and I recall watching them going down the lake and totally out of sight, cans and everything that was on there. Nothing remained, the whole outfit went.

We never did find any of the stuff that came off the trailer. We went and looked for probably 2 or 3 miles across this lake. The wind was blowing so hard that it just blew clear out of sight, it really messed my back up and I believe that I had a hairline fracture in my leg, although I never got it x-rayed. It bothered me for six to eight months. Anyway, we still had my machine and the stuff on Hank's outfit, and went up to Copper Lake. That night I suffered from the pain in my leg and back but made it through the night and bagged a couple of caribou the next day, which helped with the winter's meat supply. We cut our trip short, however, because we did not have enough supplies to last more than about a day. It was just another memorable Alaska experience that we lived to tell about. I recall having ice grousers put on the track before going out again on these lakes.

We used to go up on the Taylor Highway out of Tok, on the Alaska Highway going toward Eagle, to kill our winter supply of meat, and made many trips. All the trips I remember were quite successful. We were allowed five, or possibly six caribou back in those days, so we'd go up there and load up with these animals. They were fairly easy to get, and we got some magnificent caribou racks. Occasionally we'd pick up a moose along the way on these trips too. It was beautiful country. In recent years, they pretty much shut the hunting down up there and I think perhaps they did an overkill on the caribou, allowing that many per hunter, or they migrated out of the area, I don't know which.

I was coming back to Glennallen from Tok after delivering fuel up there one afternoon late in the year, and the moose season was still on. Driving late in the afternoon, on a turnout near Chistochina I saw a pickup and horse trailer parked there. Obviously these people were hunt-ing moose. They had a bale or two of hay in the back of the pickup and there were two bull moose, one on each side of it. One was a pretty good size bull—all bulls were legal at that time—but the other one was pretty small. They were eating hay out of the back of the pickup. There was possibly grain in there too, I don't know. There were hay bales in there, so it was one or the other. I had quite a chuckle over that. I wondered if the guys out hunting ever saw anything—they probably didn't, but they should have sat in the pickup and the moose would have come to them.

On another hunting trip late in the season in the Chistochina country, we went up there and again it was very cold, probably lower than 50 below. We broke down with our track machine, one of those Nodwell outfits, within sight of a tent camp up a little hill. We walked up to it, and there was another old-timer in the trucking business in the camp, Al Renk, whom I knew very well. He and a group were in there hunting. It was late in the afternoon, so we hunkered down in their tent and spent the night with them thanks to their hospitality, and kept from freezing to death. In the morning we were making coffee and Al asked if we wanted some bacon and eggs. I said, "You betcha." So he said, "Grab those eggs that are lying by the skirt of the tent." I went over and got them— they were like rocks, frozen solid. So Al says, "No problem." He set them in the frying pan and added some grease. This was the first time I'd ever had fried eggs in the shell, but they sure tasted good.

My son, Cliff, and another fellow, Marvin Glaze, and I went up to Northway, out of Tok on the Alaska Highway, on a duck-hunting trip in the late part of the year. It was probably about minus 20 degrees in Northway. We were going to take a little canoe and come down this little stream that was still open in the middle, with the ice along both edges. You could still navigate between the ice on each shore, so I dropped them off with the canoe and I drove the pickup back down the road about a half mile, and hoped they would scare up ducks along that stream that were migrating and landed in the river, where they would get some shooting, and as they came down the stream they would give me some shooting also. The ducks came in pretty late in the year up there, headed south, and landed in these open streams. I waited for about half an hour and heard one shot. I was standing there by the edge of the stream next to a tree, and lo and behold, I looked in the stream and an oar came floating down the river. I thought, Oh, my God, they tipped over and drowned up there in that stream. I ran back to the pickup about 50 or 60 yards uphill and grabbed a rope out of it. I tied it around the tree and around my waist. I was going to try to dive in and get them as they came floating by.

I waited and waited and nothing happened. I looked back up the road and here they came. They had gotten out of the stream up there and had been totally dunked in it. Marvin had shot at a duck right after they had got in the canoe and started down the stream. The canoe tipped over and they both tipped upside down. The guns went into the river. They managed to swim out and came walking down the road. With the temperature as low as it was, they were like zombies, their clothes frozen solid, hardly able to move their arms. So I got them into the pickup and went up to an acquaintance of mine who had a cabin and a big wood fire going. They stripped down and got thawed out.

It was quite an experience, which could have had a disastrous ending, but we made it out alright. We were even able to go back and dig the guns out later. We got the canoe back, and the whole bit, so it wasn't too bad after all,. The only thing we lost was a couple of oars.

We went out on a caribou hunting trip out of Anchorage to King Salmon, and then chartered a guide. He had a Super Cub with oversize tundra tires, and took us out and dropped us off one by one, landing on a big volcanic rock field. With these big wheels on it we set down very gently and set up our camp there. My sons, Bruce, Mike, Timothy, and Cliff, and my nephew Larry Bowen were there. We saw a lot of caribou as we flew out, there were big herds of them. It was absolutely gorgeous weather, late in the year, a little cold at night but not too bad.

Cliff Bishop with caribou antlers.

We'd been out there a day or two and had killed a couple of caribou, when about the third day a big wind came up. We were about a mile or so away from our tent, and I was sitting on a hill looking out over the tundra. The wind was really howling, and blowing harder all the time. I looked out and saw something—at first I thought it was a caribou, but then I realized it was blue in color and it was going out across the tundra. When we got back, a big wind had come up in the valley and had literally picked up the tent and blown it a good mile or more from where it had been. It was quite a mess—it had food and everything else in it, and the wind blew the whole thing with all of our gear still in it. We finally retrieved it, got it back, and certainly tied it down a lot tighter when we reset the camp. Again, it was quite an experience and a real mess.

A good friend of mine, John Besolo, my son Clifford, and I went out on a sheep-hunting trip. We went by floatplane up in the high country. It was pretty late in the afternoon so we set up camp there, and the next morning we headed up into the sheep country. It was about two in the afternoon, and we'd walked most of the day. It was a long ways up there; it was late in the year and the last part of the sheep season. It was pretty windy too and we spotted some sheep off in the distance. We decided to park our tents and sleeping bags and all our supplies there, and spread out to try and pick up one of these trophies. My son and I were together and John went off by himself. About 4 p.m. it was already getting dark. We heard John shoot a couple of shots, and Cliff and I decided we had better go back down and set up our tents and get everything set up for the night.

We got back down the hill, and it was almost dark by the time we got back down there. We looked and looked as hard as we could and could not find where we had dropped the stuff off. Anyway, we heard John shoot a couple more times, apparently for directions, so we answered and fired off several shots back and forth. About an hour and a half, possibly two hours later after dark, John showed up.

We were without any food or anything else to spend the night. We had finally given up looking for our gear. We decided we weren't going to be able to find it until daylight the next morning. The wind came up really hard, and it was very, very cold. There was nothing to burn, since we were above the timberline—no wood, the only thing was some grass. I finally decided we were going to have to do something, so I went out and started pulling up handfuls of grass and gathering small pieces of brush. Finally I got a little pile of stuff there and fired it off. I got my hands a little warmer and we took off in different directions. We kept doing this for hours on end until the next morning. We were entirely worn out, hungry, and cold. Finally, lo and behold, about 200 yards away, we found the camping gear, food, cooking stove, and all that we had brought with us. This certainly was a welcome sight.

Immediately after eating and warming up we crawled into our sleeping bags and slept for several hours. We always made a point to try to lay something out for a marker—well, this was kind of a rocky area, not much of a place you could tie anything up to in the air, but we could have laid something out on the rock, like a coat or something. Instead, we had just tossed our stuff down. Later on down the road we always marked our gear so it was easily found when we left it, which we didn't do very often. But if we had to, we took care to ensure that this would not happen again.

Chapter Twenty-Three
Fishing Alaska

Fishing in Alaska takes on many variations. For many years we were allowed to use large weighted hooks and simply cast out into the salmon-filled streams, snagging fish after fish for our winter supply. However, they put a stop to this practice as the fishing population increased and the harvest got to be very heavy in certain streams. Subsistence fishing these days relates to dipnetting using a 10- to 15-foot-long aluminum handle with a large circular or square net attached; the nets are approximately 4 feet across. This setup can be used either in a boat or off the banks of many different rivers. Each family is allotted a certain number of fish, depending on the size of the family, usually about 60 salmon for each season. I've always used a boat, because bank fishing is extremely hard work as opposed to the boat method. Most fish taken by this method are red salmon; however, on many occasions while you are dipping for reds a king salmon will hit and in most cases these huge monsters are not even slowed down. They usually break right through the netting and continue up the stream. I caught a few of the 35- or 40-pounders and landed them. Considering the fact that these fish can weigh up to nearly 100 pounds each, it would require almost a steel net to hold them.

Subsistence fishing can also be done with a set net, which is a long net weighted and placed across a section of river or near the beaches on the ocean shore. The fish simply swim into the netting and are caught by their gills. Although quite a few people fish this way, the dip-net method is by far the most popular.

Another unique method is the fish wheel. It is placed close to the riverbank and anchored to shore, usually with steel cables. It floats on pontoons or logs. This device has four big paddles and looks a lot like one of the old-time paddle-wheel riverboats. Two of the paddles are just flat with nothing attached to them, and their function is simply to contact the outgoing stream of water in the river and keep the wheel rotating, whereas the other two paddles, placed opposite each other, have huge screen baskets. As the fish swim upstream they are effectively dipped up out of the water, and with these screens sloping toward a catch box mounted on the floating deck of the wheel, the fish flop around and slide out the open end of the screen into the box. The catch is there for you on the next visit to the fishing site. I've seen these boxes filled to the point that with no room left, the fish simply slide off the top of the box and back into the water to continue their voyage upriver. We usually checked the wheels six or eight hours after setting them up. This is an effortless and efficient way to get your winter harvest, except when it comes to cleaning and processing. With 60 or more salmon you have some serious work to do. Of course, we don't want to leave out the old tried-and-true method of taking trout and salmon on rod and reel or fly-fishing for them. What a thrill fighting a huge rainbow trout or the flashing, fighting silver salmon brings! It is a real challenge hooking into the huge king salmon of 50 to 80 pounds or more.

All the above methods of taking Alaska fish are very exciting, and most of the time very rewarding, but not always. I took a trip on one of the Alaska ferries from Homer to Kodiak, the fishing capital of the world, with a friend of mine and we got three or four hours out of Homer when the weather started getting extremely rough. The farther we went the rougher it got, all the way to Kodiak. We didn't know it then, but what we were getting was the tail end of one of the worst storms in history to hit Japan. The end result was that all the fishing streams in the Kodiak area were up to flood stage and extremely muddy. Anyway, the only salmon I got after a three- or four-day fishing trip was in a restaurant in the fly-fishing capital of the world. Oh well, you don't win them all.

The king salmon is the first to run into the Kenai River after break-up. They start showing up in good numbers in May and continue through July each year. There are two runs each year, the early run and the late run. The late run has always produced the larger trophy fish; however, the world-record king was taken on May 18 in the early season by Les Anderson of Soldotna. It weighed in at 97 pounds. This big hog was caught in the early part of the first run, so you never know. A lot of the avid fishermen launch into the salt water in April near Anchor Point, Ninilchik, and Deep Creek to troll for these big kings approximately two weeks before they enter into the area rivers, and usually do quite well.

One of our favorite fish is the halibut. We look forward each year to going after these barn-door-size flatfish. We usually go out of one of the launch sites at Deep Creek or out of the harbor in Homer. At all these beach sites, they have big farm tractors, and for a small fee they hook onto your trailer with a boat on it and back it into the surf with the fishermen and all of their gear aboard. So you don't even get your feet wet. Then you take off on a big venture. You travel out for 15 or 20 miles and drop your anchor. At this point you bait the hook, usually with sardines, and then with fairly heavy weights on it because you go down 60 to 150 feet—it requires some pretty heavy weights to reach the bottom, because of the extreme tide changes—and after leaving the hook on the bottom, you kick back and wait for the first big tug on the line. After getting a fish on the work begins in earnest, depending on the size of the fish, which can be a 25- or 30-pounder, known as a chicken halibut, or one of 300 pounds or more. Any fish that weighs 60 pounds or more is referred to as a shooter, because after the fish is brought to the surface the fishermen use a small shotgun, a 410-gauge, and put a shot into its head after putting a harpoon into its body with a line attached that is tied to the boat, because these big halibut can put up a big-time fight as you get them into the boat. With all of the above actions you are assured of having fresh halibut for dinner after the day's fishing is done. Then when you get back to the beach and want to come up out of the surf the tractor backs your trailer back out into the ocean or right under the surf and you drive the boat up on it. Being high and dry, after a fun-filled day, you are safely back again.

For years we always launched in one of the small rivers such as Deep Creek, and this could only be done at or near high tide, for these small rivers were lined with rocks and the rough water could add to the problems getting your boat into the surf and out into deep water. Some fishermen used four-wheel-drive pickups and attempted to launch into the water off the sandy beaches. This usually ended with the truck getting stuck or waves tipping the boat over. It was never easy and it was a sight to behold as the fishermen, two or three of them, attempted to back into the surf with a pickup, and usually either ended up getting stuck or the boat getting tipped over, and they certainly always got wet. It made it a pretty miserable day for them. So the addition of these tractors was a great plus to the fishermen.

Chapter Twenty-Four
Bears

I recall a couple of drivers having coffee at a café when the subject of grizzly bears arose. Clyde stated that he was scared to death of running into one while out hunting and the other fellow, Mike, said that he was not one bit afraid of them but that he respected them. Clyde at this point stated that if the two of them were out hunting and a grizzly approached them on a narrow trail that he, Clyde, would climb the closest tree because of his fear and that Mike would climb the same tree because of his respect. This little conversation got a big laugh out of us.

The Forest Service had a cabin set up on Tanada Lake, up in Nabesna country. I guess it was for hiking tours and for hunters scouting the country. In any event, we heard a story that a bear had come on this cabin and attempted to break into it with a hiker inside. I went up with Doug Fredricks to look at the cabin—it was beyond belief. The bear had knocked holes into the walls on all four plywood sides of the cabin, and not only one or two but several holes, and the hiker, after being in there for an hour or so and I'm certain completely terrified—I know I would have been—with the bear threatening to break in, finally shot the bear in the chest with a pistol as it stood up in front of a window. The bear was not killed; we found blood in the snow near the cabin and tried to track it down and kill it before someone happened to run into it and be killed by it. We never did find that bear. We assumed, of course, that it had died somewhere. I'm sure it did. It was a traumatic experience for that fellow, this monstrous bear trying to get to him. It certainly showed the force they have. I was totally impressed by it.

A fellow by the name of Timothy Treadwell was here in Alaska every year.

Every summer he came up and actually went out and lived amongst the bears out in the Katmai Preserve. There was a lot of controversy over the way he interacted with these bears. He would actually crawl up to them with his camera turned on and he described them as nothing but great big teddy bears, and harmless. He never carried a gun, not even pepper spray, and actually got away with this for several years much to the surprise of a lot of people. He had a lot of support from the Hollywood stars who donated money to his so-called wildlife studies. His study, as he called it, went on for several years. I believe it was in 2003 that the papers announced that he and his girlfriend, Amy Huguenard, who was with him, were eaten by a bear, obviously a fatal mistake. These teddy bears have very sharp teeth and claws and you may have to wait for a while, but eventually a bear will come along that will view you as no more than a walking pork chop, and have no second thoughts about helping himself to a meal.

A guide on Snowshoe Lake near Glennallen had located a bear's den in the country near there, in the Eureka area. He called a fellow in Anchorage who wanted to kill a bear, so the guy came out and they flew in there in his Super Cub, went into where the den was and waited and waited. Nothing showed up. They didn't see the bear, so the guy decided to take a pole and put it down into the hole and try to get the bear to come out—at least that was a scenario presented after the fact. Whether that actually happened nobody really knows. What they didn't know was that the bear was on a little knoll 50 yards from them and had been lying there all the time watching from his vantage point. Suddenly, the bear came charging down and killed both the guide and the hunter. Whitey Fassler, an old friend of mine and a longtime guide at Gunsight Mountain Lodge, went out with a Fish and Wildlife man after the bodies were recovered, to kill the bear. Whitey told me that when they got there trees were torn up in a large area around where this had happened—the bear was really angry. They finally located the bear and it charged them. When they shot and killed it, it was on a hard charge and no more than 20 feet from them as it dropped. Truly a ferocious bear, and one bent on destroying anything that came into its domain. Whitey had this bear mounted and it was in the Gunsight Mountain Lodge on the Glenn Highway for years.

Another fellow by the name of Newt Peterson, who lived in Tok, went out to visit a friend who lived about a quarter mile off the Glenn Highway, in a cabin. Newt started walking down toward the cabin and was no more than about 200 yards off the road when a grizzly bear attacked him. He was terribly mauled; it took 7 or 8 months to recuperate from this. He spent approximately three months in the hospital and was terribly scarred. I saw him many times after that; he had terrible scars on his face and arms and was close to being killed by this bear. You never know where they might be, either out in the wild or 50 yards from where you're walking off the road. It's not a good idea to go anywhere in the outlying area without a gun in your hand, in my opinion.

Another incident occurred in the Glennallen area when a guy named Happy flew a New York hunter out. They took off in a floatplane on a moose-hunting trip. They spotted a bear on the way out and decided to land the plane and make a stalk on him. They walked to where they had seen the bear after landing on this lake—it is totally illegal to do this because you're not supposed to hunt the same day you're airborne. In any event, they walked to where they spotted the moose kill the bear was on and went cautiously in that direction. The bear would not show himself till after half an hour or so. Happy said, "You wait here and I'll go ahead and try to get the bear to rise up, so get ready to shoot." Happy went ahead and the bear, in fact, was there and charged head-on into him. The New York hunter fired at the bear and missed him, and Happy was killed by the bear. The New Yorker ran as hard as he could back to where the plane was at the lake and managed to get the radio to work. He radioed Glennallen airport of the circumstances. Fish and Wildlife came out and killed the bear and recovered Happy's body. There was quite a furor over it, because they charged the New York hunter with illegally hunting the game on the same day as being airborne. But I guess he wasn't too discouraged about that—the very fact that he didn't lose his life was much more important than the charges.

There was an incident at Laird Hot springs on the Alcan Highway. It's a very popular place really close to the road. A black bear came into the hot springs when a woman and her son were swimming there, got a hold of the woman and killed her. A man attempting a rescue was also killed. The young son hit the bear over the head with a limb and Dwayne Engleberg came along, got a gun from someone, and went in and killed the bear. Dwayne was on his way to Alaska when this happened.

Al Lee is a guide on the Glenn Highway out of Glennallen. He had a cabin there across a little lake. A man and his wife went over to this cabin in a boat and were working on repairs to the roof. A black bear came out as they were up on the roof. The bear was there for an hour or so, circling around trying to get at them. The man finally decided when the bear got on the other side of the house, he'd drop the ladder which he had pulled onto the roof to keep the bear from climbing, come down the ladder as fast as he could, run and jump in the boat, and row back over to get his rifle to kill the bear. I guess he knocked the ladder to the ground when he got off the roof to keep the bear from climbing it, so there was no ladder for the bear to crawl up on. The bear, in the meantime, crawled up a tree that was adjacent to the house, dropped down on the roof, and knocked the woman off it. She had been partially eaten by the time he got back with his gun. It was a tragic situation. And this was a black bear and not a grizzly, so you never know.

Many visitors, when they come to Alaska for the first time, arrive with little idea of what awaits them: living conditions, do people really live in igloos, are dog teams the mode of transportation, and many preconceived wrong ideas. An example; I was working at the Hub of Alaska in Glennallen in the service station when a man came in with his vehicle's right head lamp dangling by the attached wires. He rushed over to where we were visiting with a couple of friends.

"I just ran over a polar bear," he exclaims!

This got our immediate attention. We all knew that the nearest polar bear habitat was 700 miles north on the Arctic Ocean. We asked the man, "where did this happen?"

He said, "about three miles back down the road."

We got into my pickup and went to see for ourselves. Sure enough, when we got to the spot, we discovered a very dead, medium sized black bear.

The visitor had been taught that Alaska was where there were polar bears, so he had run over and killed a polar bear—regardless of its size, shape, or color.

Chapter Twenty-Five
Avalanches

Filling in for one of my drivers on the Alyeska turbine fuel haul, I had loaded up at the topping plant at Isabel Pass and was headed down to Pump 12 on the Richardson Highway. I was traveling only 35 to 40 miles per hour at about mile 208 at 2 a.m. when an avalanche came in on my left side and just barely ahead of the truck. I couldn't stop in time to keep from running into it and hit full on into this pile of snow so hard that the front end of the truck was elevated and it ended up stopped at about a 20-degree angle. Actually, the front end had gone right up over the top of the thing; it settled back down into the snow, and for several feet it came to a stop. With the weight of a fully loaded rig pressing down on it, there was a perfect mold of both the underside of the truck and trailer. This resulted in almost six hours of working on it after the snow removal equipment showed up a couple of hours later. This outfit was pressed down into the snow so hard that it basically turned to ice, and the end result of all the shaking and pushing on the equipment was that every spring on the truck had broken leafs and had to be replaced. I guess I was lucky that I didn't get hit broadside, since it most certainly would have shoved me off the road and buried the whole outfit.

Jack Wallace was caught in an avalanche and told me that his truck was totally covered but had stayed on the road, and while sitting inside he could hear the road equipment working on clearing the snow away, and hope that a bulldozer blade wouldn't rip into his cab before they discovered his truck hidden underneath this huge pile of snow. What Jack didn't know was that the only thing showing was a little of his exhaust pipe sticking up out of the snow, so they knew that there was a rig buried underneath, and cleared it all away without doing any damage to Jack or his truck. He said he tried to blow his air horn, and being jam-packed with snow it wouldn't work, so he kept stepping on his brakes hoping they would hear the air exhaust until all the air was gone. He was a happy fellow for surviving the avalanche and the removal, not hurting anything, especially him.

The overwhelming force of an avalanche is hard for a person to imagine. We think of snow as nice, soft flakes floating down out of the sky or to take a sled ride or ski on, but one of these monsters comes down off a steep slope and there are very few things that can stand in its way and not be destroyed. I recall a road crew working on the Seward Highway alongside the Turnagain Arm clearing the highway of an avalanche when another one came down, and struck the bulldozer square in the side. It went tumbling and rolling across the mud flats adjacent to the road and killed the operator—a tragic event, but one that is very possible in many areas throughout Alaska. Fortunately, in most of these no one gets hurt. It is a fact that every winter skiers, snowmachiners, and cross-country skiers get caught up in avalanches, and unfortunately every year there are those few who don't survive.

A few years back several of the Grand kids came to Alaska for the holidays and decided to go to Alyeska ski resort for a day of skiing and snowboarding. They left Soldotna in the morning and the weather was fine; however, by the time the day was over it had turned real nasty with high winds and blowing snow. They got on the Seward Highway and headed down the road toward home with visibility practically nonexistent, and after what seemed like a long ways they thought they had passed the turnoff from the Seward Highway to the Sterling Highway, which goes back to Soldotna, so they decided to stop at the next road sign they came to, and try to get an idea where they were. In a short while they saw a snow-covered sign and stopped. One of the kids got out and with a swipe of the hand knocked the snow from the sign, and there in very bold letters it stated DO NOT STOP AVALANCHE AREA.

The car was already moving as the young man raced back to jump in and departed the area. They had only gotten to around Summit Lake and were still a few miles short of their turnoff. They finally made it home all worn out but safe and sound after their day in the snow. It was kind of funny after the fact but not at the time he read the sign.

A tragic event occurred in Turnagain Pass on the Seward Highway where snowmachine riders were caught up in a massive slide that stretched for over a mile along the mountain range and resulted in seven riders losing their lives, basically as a result of being in the wrong place at the wrong time. These past events have prompted avalanche experts to predict slides, and give warnings, and I'm certain this is a great help in keeping people from getting hurt or killed. In the winter of 1959, Alaska Freight Lines was running into Valdez, and there had been a heavy snowfall with extreme avalanche conditions. It seems that the regular driver was sick and so Art Erickson took the trip for him. Three trucks were making the same trip, and Art was running behind the other two rigs. An avalanche occurred at about milepost 36 on the Richardson Highway between Art and the other two rigs, which had already gotten through ahead of him.

Art stopped, and looking the situation over, knew it would be a long wait for road equipment to arrive to open the road so he backed up far enough to be out of the way of the upcoming removal operation. He crawled into the sleeper when another avalanche came down and he was sitting right in its path. It shoved his fully loaded truck into the canyon below and killed him. The other drivers knew that he was behind them, and when the slide was cleaned out and he had not shown up they started the search that discovered his buried rig, a very unfortunate situation, and one that can occur at any time in many places in Alaska.

Chapter Twenty-Six
Alaska Flying Experiences

We had a 206 Cessna airplane that was used in the business for flying parts and personnel around; because of the vast area we operated over, and with support services mainly in Anchorage and Fairbanks, this plane became a very valuable help in getting drivers and equipment back on the road when the need arose. Many times we had a breakdown that was so far away from a shop facility that it would have required a tow truck or lowboy and besides

Bruce Bishop and Bishop Trucking Cessna 206.

the time element, a huge cost to get the rig fixed. With the plane we simply flew the parts in, along with a mechanic, landed the plane on the road, and it was soon back in service. There were occasions when the plane happened to be traveling to or from our Interior operations area when they were called upon to act as an air ambulance.

Our pilot Steph Strunk was flying from Glennallen to Anchorage on one occasion and observed a car wreck on the road near Eureka. He proceeded to land on the road nearby and took a couple of badly injured people to the hospital emergency room in Anchorage. They were very grateful for the help. On several other occasions we were able to lend a helping hand in emergencies. The recreational activities the plane allowed us to enjoy were many and varied—hunting, fishing, and traveling over vast areas of our beautiful state. We had a cabin at Lake Clark that we had built over the years, and used to fly out there for weekends—wonderful fishing and beautiful country.

The plane was set up on floats in the summertime, and my son Bruce and Steph Strunk were the main pilots; they would never let me fly the plane when they were around. So they did the flying, and on one occasion at Port Alsworth, a small inlet off Lake Clark with several houses and cabins along the shore, they were getting ready to take off, with my son Bruce as the pilot, just offshore waiting for the last passenger to get in the plane. With no one else there at the time, this fellow took our jet boat 30 or 40 feet out from shore to the plane so he wouldn't get his shoes and pants wet. The guy got into the plane and Bruce started to take off, and the people on shore were waving to them so they waved back. Bruce idled on toward the opening of the little inlet into the main lake and gave the plane full throttle to take off, but it wouldn't go. What happened was that this guy had tied the plane onto the float strap and they were towing the boat along with the plane. The people on shore had been trying to wave them down and, of course, laughing all the time at this bunch of dummies with their tagalong jet boat. They were pretty embarrassed when bringing the boat back to the cabin where it belonged.

I had a friend who had a floatplane. When I told him I was going to tell of his mishap he made me promise not to print his name. Seems he had dropped off a couple of friends who were hunting at a remote Alaska lake. While getting their gear to shore, the plane was not tied down, a gust of wind blew the plane onto the lake. It was far enough out by the time they noticed that there was no way it could be retrieved. The plane hung up a few yards from shore on the other side of the lake. The end result was that it took more than 24 hours of walking around the lake and then getting very wet and cold. My friend assured me that this would never happen again.

Chapter Twenty-Seven
Truck Experiences

After selling the bulk plant, I got involved with Darrell LaMonica, the ex-Oakland Raiders quarterback, who had leased the operating authority of Arctic Motor Freight. We began hauling for Alyeska Pipeline, delivering freight to the North Slope from Anchorage and Fairbanks, and since we were running back south empty, Alyeska offered us a contract to pick up loads of surplus material on the pipeline corridor that had been used in the construction of the line and we modified half a dozen trailers per their request to accompany these loads. After picking up the first two loads I got a call in Anchorage at my office to come to Fairbanks and meet with two individuals involved with this large movement. One was from the construction company and the other from Alyeska Corporation. I drove up to Fairbanks the next day thinking that this meeting was to discuss the logistics of this ongoing haul. When I arrived in Fairbanks and called for directions to the meeting place I was told to come to a business building instead of the construction company office. When I arrived at the designated spot I was met by only one of the two individuals, the man from the construction company. I was shocked to learn from him that if I wished to continue with this haul I would have to pay 10% of the gross pay in cash for each load. My immediate reaction was—what happens if Alyeska finds out? His answer was that one of the higher-ups at Alyeska was involved and I was to meet him the next day at this same spot at a predetermined time. I agreed.

I flew back to Anchorage that night and contacted Alyeska headquarters in Anchorage, and was told to meet them that same evening, which I did. At this meeting there were probably seven or eight people, and I told them of this plan. However, I did not know the name of the Alyeska person I was to meet the next day. They asked if I would meet this person while wearing a wire. I agreed. At 8 a.m. the next day I met again at the Alyeska building and was fitted with a wire setup. A couple of hours later I went up to Fairbanks. I didn't know if this fellow would be suspicious and would want to pat me down. I figured if he did I would simply turn and walk out, and if that failed it would be me against him and so I was prepared for just about anything. However, there was no problem along these lines. In my meeting I asked his reasons for doing this, since obviously he had a good job and was making good pay. He said the whole thing was a short-lived deal—the pipeline—and his only interest in it was the money. He came right out and asked if I agreed to pay the specified amount and my answer was yes, because we had gone to a lot of expense in modifying the trailers and wanted the haul very badly. I didn't know how to get his name, when he gave me one of his business cards and told me to call him when the next load arrived. He would go to our office in Fairbanks and pick up the cash for the first two loads hauled and the third one also. I could not believe how brazen he was about this whole thing.

I went back to Anchorage and was met by the same group as the night before and found out that five of them were lawyers, representing each of the five partners making up the Alyeska Pipeline Company, and the others were high-ranking officials of the company. The end result of this whole fiasco was that the construction company lost the loading contract and we never did get any of these loads. Later on, Alyeska fired this employee. He later sued them and I got called in as a witness by Alyeska and did depositions to these happenings. Down the road he lost the lawsuit and all he got out of it was the smearing of his name. I'm sure he never worked for another oil company again. All I got out of it was threatening to be shot by the guy at the construction company and fired by Alyeska. All of this operation was short-lived and very costly to me.

Chapter Twenty-Eight
Bishop Trucking

We still had a half dozen trucks and trailers and with the shutting down of Arctic Motor Freight, I purchased the Alaska Transportation Commission operating authority of Arctic Motor Freight and started hauling with the tanker authority, operating as Bishop Trucking Inc., hauling fuel for the Chevron oil company, the U.S. Army, and other customers. One of the first jobs we took on after starting our operation was with a chemical company in Anchorage that had a contract with Alyeska Pipeline Services Company to supply a product called Tri Ethelene Glycol, which was to be shipped from Anchorage to Prudhoe Bay on the North Slope. This product was loaded on the tankers at approximately 75 degrees Fahrenheit, and it was necessary to keep it very near that temperature during shipment. When cooled off it jells up and cannot be pumped, but after water is added it is like automotive antifreeze and will not freeze up. Alyeska did not want to pay to ship the product with the water added, since they would be paying twice the freight, so without freezing we had to get it up to Prudhoe Bay, where they would add the water to it. We took a big gamble and had three tankers built with water lines running through the inside bottom of the tanks, and then plumbed the radiators on the trucks to connect to these lines, thereby circulating hot water through the load. This product arrived in Prudhoe at or above its temperature when loaded in Anchorage. This saved many thousands of dollars.

Alyeska also had a need to transport fuel from their topping plants, where they refined turbine fuel from the oil in the pipeline. This product was transported to the pump stations to fuel the large turbine engines that generated power to pump the crude oil from Prudhoe Bay to Valdez, and was then shipped on tankers to refineries in the contiguous United States. Going from a privately owned business such as the Union Oil bulk plant that we had operated for several years, to Bishop Trucking, Inc., a common carrier, was like going from day to night. It required being subjected to all kinds of rules and regulations that we soon found out to be heavily influenced by politics and heavy-handed business practices. The trucking companies in those days were operated either under the Alaska Transportation Commission, the Interstate Commerce Commission, or both.

We operated under the Alaska Transportation Commission and soon found that everything we did was overseen by this agency, and if any changes to our permit were desired it was necessary to file for these changes through this agency, during which time you could be assured that at least one and nearly always five or six of your competitors filed an opposition to

A typical Bishop Trucking tanker.

whatever your request happened to be. These actions always required you to have a good transportation attorney in your corner. We filed a request for extension of authority to haul loads from Valdez to the Alaska Interior. Our existing permit allowed us to haul into Valdez from most of the state but precluded us from hauling loads back out of there. Chevron wanted us to haul for them from Valdez to several of their bulk plants throughout the Interior. After filing for this extension we waited for the hearing to be scheduled, and at that time, we presented our case, with our attorney, in front of a hearing officer and at the Alaska Transportation Commission headquarters in Anchorage. We were opposed by several of our competitors, but were optimistic that since we had a long-term existing contract going into Valdez our request would be approved with no problem. It was the wrong approach, because it didn't take more than a few days for us to be notified that our request was denied. We were left totally bewildered by this unforeseen action but had no recourse. These three commissioners were the final answer to all transportation questions within the state.

My attorney, John Wood, was a very thorough young man and took it upon himself to go back up to the commission office a few days later and make a formal written request to the office staff for all the records of this recently held hearing. John called my office and told me to get to his office as soon as possible after he had been up there and that he had big news for me. When I arrived he said, "Look at this," and showed me a copy he had made of a ledger, showing that the commissioners had signed to remove the hearing documents to review them when they were back in town from wherever they were and then to make a decision on this hearing. Since all the commissioners were out of town, a hearing officer was assigned to oversee and hold this meeting in their absence. The only thing missing was the signature of any one of the politically appointed individuals to remove these documents, and none of them had ever even seen any of the documents or heard one word of the testimony—yet the answer to our request was a resounding no. Needless to say, the following day our approval for extension was granted. The bias of these individuals was clear. We could have hung them by the nearest rafter if they had not granted our authority after John discovered what they had done, and we would have done that for certain. The beginning of the end of this body came after a massive effort by this same attorney, John Wood, who kept after them until they were effectively removed by a sunset action of the State. Obviously, these commissioners were biased, and made their decisions based on what some of our competitors wanted, not on facts.

This Alyeska haul on the turbine fuel was divided between three or four of the trucking companies. Alyeska Pipeline Services Company decided to put their haul up for bid to a single company over a three-year period. The equipment used at the time by all the carriers was either a tractor running a 40-foot semitank trailer with a total of seven axles between two pieces of equipment or a truck and trailer with seven or eight total axles. These rigs, set up as described, could legally haul approximately 8,000 to 9,500 gallons. One of the things that had a large impact on a year-round contract was the annual weight reduction imposed by the State of Alaska during the so-called break-up period, when temperatures were up from the subzero range of winter and roadbeds started to thaw. During this period, heavily loaded trucks can cause severe damage to the roads and therefore the loads are restricted, in most cases to 75% of the normal maximum allowable load, and on occasion to as low as 50%. This doesn't happen very often, and usually not on the main roads. This meant that for an 8,000-, 8,300-gallon normal payload at 75% max load, we could get only 5,000 or 6,000 gallons across the scales, depending on the weight of the equipment and the number of axles. I decided to bid this contract based on equipment set up with a total of twelve axles—four on the tractor, three on each of the two semitrailers, and two axles for the rear semitrailer. With this configuration, and a total overall length of approximately 120 feet, we could get 14,000 gallons per load across the scales year-round. This allowed us to reduce the cents per gallon by a large margin, thereby providing savings to the Alyeska oil company, and still maintain a healthy profit margin for ourselves. In so doing we were able to outbid the competition and secure this contract. With the winning of this contract we felt certain that we would be hauling fuel for Alyeska for many years, based on our concept, and especially that at the end of this initial three-year period the tankers would all be paid for and on the next round of bids we could lower our rates even more and still retain a healthy profit margin. I was 100% correct in that these tankers have indeed carried all the turbine fuel for many years, but they were not operated by Bishop Trucking, Inc.

We had a letter from the manufacturers that they would deliver the 20 tankers within 30 days of placement of the order. Approximately two weeks after we placed the order, we got another letter from them stating that because of assembly-line problems they would be shutting down for a period of three months. I immediately got in touch with them and informed them of the 30-day commitment I had received. Their reply was that they had never sent such a letter. We searched our office many times but were never able to come up with this commitment letter; it had apparently been lost at the office. It had been written by a salesman; it was his personal guarantee and not the company's. However, had I found the letter, it would automatically have been binding on the company, because he was representing the company. Unfortunately we could not find it and he was not about to admit that he wrote it for fear of getting fired. After all was said and done, we tried to get other trailer companies to build our specialized equipment, but none of them could get it built as close to the time frame as these people could even with the three-month delay. Besides that, the financing was all set up with them and we pretty much had to go along with the situation, despite the fact that we didn't like it. We bit our tongues and waited and it was a full six months before our trailers were delivered. We operated at a loss all this time by having to use our old equipment that carried a payload of only 8,500 gallons at a much reduced rate, because our bid was based on having our new equipment in place and hauling more payload.

In any event, after a short period of time we were starting to show signs of pulling out of this hole when a much bigger problem arose. The insurance company had raised our rates to astronomical heights;

this was not done by only one or two insurance companies, but all the big outfits. I've been told that it was due to the big drop in interest rates. Those companies raised their rates to offset their bottom line—windfall profits, in other words. I personally think it was called greed, and it raised our rates from $160,000 per year to $680,000 per year overnight. This sort of reminded me of petroleum prices—they don't need to justify it, they just do it.

With our insurance about to be canceled I had an offer from a company called Progressive Transport to take over our contract and keep ten of our new tractors leased for the duration of the contract, at which time they would be paid off. They could continue operating under this existing contract because they were self-insured and weren't affected by the spike in insurance premiums. We had an attorney draw up this agreement for the sale of Bishop Trucking Company and after leaving his office, this company representative took it upon himself to go back and tell the attorney to put in a 30-day cancellation clause on my trucks, without my knowledge. We had only one attorney, which was a big mistake. I thought I was dealing with honorable people, and signed this contract on the sale of the company without reading it. Since we had no issues in any area and had a clear-cut and understandable handshake deal, I didn't find out that the contract had been altered until about 30 days later when my trucks were laid off. Upon raising hell about it, I found out that I had indeed cut my own throat by signing this document. I was unable to get this action reversed and basically lost everything I had over my own stupidity. After another couple of years, some unauthorized dealings between the carrier and someone in the company came to light, and they no longer kept the contract. I understand there was some jail time for illegal actions by some of the principals of this company, having to do with employee withholdings or other federal violations. So much for dealing with bandits. My concept of utilizing this equipment had saved many hundreds of thousands of dollars over the years, and also made the operators of the equipment large profits—unfortunately for me, a set of circumstances kept me from enjoying anything but the heartache of it.

Chapter Twenty-Nine
Hauling Lumber

After finding ourselves out of the highly competitive Alaska trucking business and with a couple of Kenworths not doing anything, we decided to start hauling lumber out of Canada and started a lumber yard in Wasilla.

I was hauling out of Kitwanga, B.C. I took my 17-year-old son, Tim, with me and we left Wasilla and arrived in Kitwanga 35 or 40 hours later. I had gotten very little sleep, and had dozed over the wheel a couple of times. We loaded up and I was totally out of eyeballs. The road was very flat between Kitwanga and Mezziadan Junction, so I asked Tim if he would like to drive. Of course, the answer was an enthusiastic yes, for I had been teaching him to drive on certain sections of the roads that were not in the mountains and suited to a beginner. So away we went and with everything going real smooth I crawled back into the sleeper to catch a couple of hours of much-needed rest. When I awoke, we were sitting at the junction of Highway 37 and the Alaska Highway, near Watson Lake. I had been asleep for nine hours or better. This was the start of a career in driving on the road for Tim that today measures several million miles and he is still going strong hauling here in Alaska over the entire state and the Haul Road to Prudhoe Bay. After the lumberyard operation ran its course(went broke) I found myself watching entirely too much television, and decided to rectify this situation by renewing my CDL Class A license and going back to driving again for someone else. My first job was driving from Anchorage to Seattle and returning each week. I ran this with a codriver as a sleeper team, and after being away from these long runs for some time, it took a bit of getting used to again.

To leave Seattle with freight, several road options are available. Many, many times truckers choose to go on the road from Prince George to Prince Rupert. At Kitwanga the highway goes north up to Watson Lake. It cuts off over a hundred miles of distance, and I personally preferred going that way although the area had a tremendous snowfall. Nonetheless, a lot of us used that road, and it had some very narrow bridges. By now they have all been replaced and it's a beautiful trip through there, through Kitwanga up through Mezziadan Junction, up to Bell 1 and Bell 2, which are river crossings, and to Dease Lake half-way up to Watson Lake. It was a great trip. The other option was going straight from Prince George up the Hart Highway to Dawson Creek and taking the Alcan Highway toward Fort St. John and on to Watson Lake, Whitehorse, and Alaska. Preference didn't matter—lots of times there was a storm on one road or the other; you always checked the road conditions at Prince George. Sometimes the road was closed on the Cassiar and we'd have to go the other way, and vice versa. They had some avalanches and heavy snow and that type of thing, so we always made a decision at Prince George which way we were going to go.

I ran with Ron DeRosset, Fred Pineo, and Keith Hackey, all long-time Alaskan drivers. I believe they all had some doubts about running with an 80-year-old codriver, but they went along without too much resistance. After several months, I was running full-time with Keith Hackey. Fred Pineo was driving another company truck. Keith and I were heading south as usual, traveling from Watson Lake to Kitwanga on Highway 37, the Cassiar, this being our favorite route to Seattle. It was in the middle of winter, and of course, the road was covered in ice, but we were getting decent traction since the weather was very cold. I was driving and Keith had just crawled out of the sleeper and was sitting in the jump seat when I saw a row of truck lights. I couldn't figure it out at first, but in the same instant I viewed a large obstruction in the road. I immediately backed off the throttle, at which time my Jake brake engaged. The roadbed was so slick that the engine started to die because the drivers quit turning when the Jake brake engaged. I touched the throttle, shut the Jake brake off at the same instant, and gently touched the brakes. The immediate result was that the trailer swung to one side in the first stage of a jackknife. I got back on the throttle and got the tractor and trailer back into a straight line, all of this happening within a very short distance. By this time I could see that a vehicle was lying on its side in the middle of the road. What had happened was that this vehicle had turned over and spilled fuel all over the road, and when a northbound truck came upon the accident, he slowed way down to see if anyone was still inside. When he started to back up, his drive tires were sitting on some of the spilled fuel and he spun out on the little hill. In backing up to try and get a run at it, his trailer crossed the road.

We arrived just as he was trying to get started again, and of course, here we came, not knowing that we were running into the same area where this 1-ton diesel had rolled over going in the same direction as we were, and spilling fuel the whole way clear up to where he had stopped and beyond. This created an extremely dangerous situation, since I had no idea whether or not this accident had just happened. The thought flashed through my mind that there might be people still inside this overturned rig, so my very first thought was to avoid hitting it at all costs. I had to make an instantaneous decision to try and miss it on the left or right side. Seeing a big drop on the right side of the road, I chose the left side, all the time holding the throttle in neutral position, neither letting off nor applying any throttle. This allowed the rig to stay in a straight line once we straightened out. Looking ahead 30 or 40 yards from this overturned vehicle, I could see that the other truck and trailer were at roughly a 45-degree angle across the road, with drive tires turning rapidly, although it appeared that the rig was sitting still. So I aimed at the back of his trailer and got back to the right side of the road as far as possible without dropping off, and by the grace of the good Lord, I missed the back of his trailer by fractions of an inch and was able to stay on the road after passing him.

The irony of this whole thing was having my company codriver, Keith, sitting there observing this whole escapade. In the other truck was Fred Pineo, driving the only other truck belonging to M&M that was on the road between Anchorage and Seattle at this time, a rare fact indeed, and one that none of us will soon forget. Had I hit this rig, it would have very effectively put this company out of business and very probably would have resulted in major injuries or worse to those of us involved. I was very thankful that it turned out as it did. I decided that maybe it was time to do something that required a lot less energy than fighting these roads and living out of a sleeper, leaving it for someone much younger than I. Besides that, I had reached a milestone in that as far as I could determine, I was the oldest driver by a large margin still driving the Alaska Highway, a record that I had no desire to maintain. On one of my last trips on the Alcan I overheard a couple of Alaskan drivers talking to each other on their radios and was paying little or no attention to them when I heard my name mentioned, which immediately got my full attention. The conversation went something like this: The number one driver stated that on his last trip he had run across Cliff Bishop at one of the truck stops on the Alcan Highway and was very surprised that Cliff was still driving. The other guy came back and stated "Hell, I thought he was 90 years old several years back." Needless to say, this got my attention and I decided to throw in the towel. I sold my truck, and ironically, on the first trip south by the new owners, it was wrecked and totally destroyed. I don't know whether this would have happened had I been driving it. I sort of hoped it wouldn't have but that is, in fact, what occurred. After a lifetime of trucking, and turning to age 82, I became restless and started a retail lumberyard in Soldotna, Alaska, and oh yes—I have reinstated my CDL (commercial driver's license). I'm hauling loads of lumber throughout Alaska. It beats the hell out of sitting on my duff and watching TV. I've got an old Ford diesel with a 3406 Cat engine with a 53-foot flatbed trailer. I must admit that I am enjoying it a lot. Maybe at age ninety I'll make a sincere effort to retire.

Or not.

Appendix A
Alaskan Drivers and Old-Timers

Abercrombie, Major
Able, Lawrence
Acker, Don
Adams, Dean
Adams, Dick
Adams, Frank
Adams, Kieth
Adams, Lee
Ahgook, Jack
Aklestad,Ron
Allen, Ward
Allenbaum, Mark
Allenbaum, Mark
Amands, Lauren St
Anderson, A.J.
Anderson, Andy
Anderson, Andy Jr.
Anderson, Chuck
Anderson, Jack
Anderson, Lloyd
Anderson, Merle
Anderson, Ron
Anderson, Vic
Andrew, Floyd Jr.
Armstrong, Jeff
Arnell, Les
Arnett, Leo
Arnold, Rich
Asay, Richard, Allen
Athey, Dick

Aubel, Marty
Auble, Malcomb
Austen, James
Austin, Gene
Austin, Scotty
Bachner, Jess
Baggs, Dale
Bagley, ?
Bailey, Herb
Baily, Dan
Baker, Bob
Baker, Lee
Bane, Lowell
Barber, Bruce
Barber, Dale
Barber, Jack
Barber, Jim
Barbie, Don
Barite, Hoagy
Barkhuff, Dale
Barner, Conrad
Barnes, Russ
Barr, Betty
Barr, Charley
Barr, Frank
Barr, Larry
Barr, Leroy
Barry, Dick
Bart, Lewis
Bartholomew, Ralph

Bates, Lee
Batey, Bob
Bauer, Ray
Bayless, Bill
Bayless, Howard
Bayless, Otto
Beals, Roger
Bear, Leo
Beaudoin, Blake
Beaudoin, Doug (Digger)
Beaudoin, Lucky
Beaver, Roy
Beck, James
Beckham, Chuck
Bederman, Horace
Belton, Charles
Bender, Alvin
Bennett, Gary
Bennett, Terry
Berger, Bob
Berger, Rod
Berght, Neil
Berry, Dick
Berzinski, Jim
Biggs, Dale
Biggs, Larry
Billingslea, Earl
Binger, Brian
Bishop, Bruce
Bishop, Cliff

Bishop, Cliff 3rd
Bishop, Jeanne
Bishop, Mike
Bishop, Sam
Bishop, Skeet
Bishop, Tim
Bishop, Tom
Bivens, John
Bizzet, Mike
Blackard, Danny
Blackard, Joe
Blackwell, Jess
Bland, Earl
Blaton, Don
Boggs, Kennith
Bohanon, Glenn
Booky, James
Bottom,Grayson
Bouillion, Dick
Bowden, Clare
Bowen, Lance
Bowen, Larry
Bowers, Duane
Bowler, Don
Bowman, Virgil
Bradbury, Max
Bradford, Ronny
Bradley, Clayton
Bradstreet, Allan
Brand, Tom
Branson, Bill
Bredemeyer, Tary
Brewer, Percy
Brewster, Bob
Brewster, Dick
Bridgers, John
Briggs, Walt
Brigman, Nick
Briton, Bill
Britt, R. L.
Brooks, Earl
Brooks, Larry
Brosti, Jerry
Brown, Charley
Brown, Dick
Brown, Don

Brown, Ed
Brown, Freddy
Brown, Larry
Brown, Stan
Brown, Ted
Brown, Tom
Browning, Jim
Browning, Joe
Bruce, Jack
Bruce, Joe
Buck, Carl
Buck, G.E.
Buck, John
Buck, Mel
Buck, Ted
Bullock, Chuck
Burger, Don
Burgess, Lee
Burke, Jim
Burnison, Bill
Butcher, Nat
Butchlar, Harold
Buzzby, Bill
Cable, Ron
Cadigan, Pat
Cadwell, Don
Caldwell, Gary
Calton, Al
Cambell, Don
Cambell, Jerry
Cambell, Sid
Cameron, Dan
Campbell, Jerry
Carbon, Francis
Carl, George
Carlisle, Scotty
Carlson, Al
Carlson, Bill
Carlson, Bob
Carmichael, Jack
Carr, Jess
Carr, Joe
Carr, John
Carter, Willie
Castor, Roy
Cavallero, Bob

Cavanaugh, Orville
Cecil, James
Chadwick, Gil
Chadwick, Orville
Chafee, Hugh
Chamberlin, C
Chambers, Butch
Chapados, Frank
Chapman, Shelby
Charley, Earnie
Charley, Jerry
Chatfield, John
Chicks, Ted
Childress, Joe
Christanson, Bert
Christanson, George
Christensen, Curt
Christenson, Chris
Christoferson, Fred
Ckayhill, Tom
Clark, Arnold
Clark, Austin
Clark, Dolores
Clark, John
Clark, Paul
Clark, R.C.
Clark, Red
Clements, Tom
Cobb, Art
Cochran, Jessie
Cochran, Ray
Cole, Paul
Cole, Tom
Coleman, Barry
Coleman, Ken
Collins, Lem
Conard, Hugh
Conkle, Bud
Conkle, Colin
Connely, Jerry
Conner, Junior
Conners, Hugh
Connley, Bill
Conrad, Hugh
Conway, Ron
Cook, Bill

Cook, Pat
Coolidge, Hank
Cooper, Bob
Coor, Dalton
Copeland, Al
Courtney, Al
Cowell, Claude
Cox, Dick
Cox, Larry
Cox, Mike
Craig, Shannon
Cranor, Lonnie (Shagnasty)
Cranor, Peggy
Crawford, Bill
Crockett, James
Cross, Tom
Crosswell, Allan
Crowder, Robert
Crowe, Bill
Crowell, Melvin
Crump, Jerry
Cruthers, Curt
Cuddle, Fred
Cummings, Jerry
Curiis, Barry
Curl, Larry
Curt, Jerry
Curt, John
Curtis, Larry
Daly, Rich
Daughenbaugh, Ivan
Daughenbaugh, Rick
Daught, Ed
Daumer, Earl
Dauphet, Ed
Davenport, Al
Davies, Roland
Davis, Tom
Day, Bobby
Dean, Earl
Dean, George
Decker, Dean
DeGross, Ray
DeLong, Slim
Demeritt, Del
Dempsey, Hiram

Dempsey, Jack
DeRossett, Paul
DeRossett, Ron
Derrick, Ferril
Dewitt, Martin
DeYoung, Dick
Diaz, Ray
Dickson, Orin
Dieringer, Roy
Diesinger, Roy
Dilley, Dave
Dillon, Dave
Dillon, Roy
Dinek, A. T.
Dismonte, George
Ditman, Bob
Ditmer, Dave
Dixon, Warren
Dohrman, Earnest
Downs, Robert
Doyle, Jim
Doyle, Jimmy
Dozett, Mike
Drugland, Bob
Drummond, Gary
Drurry, Joe
Dunn, Arron
Dunn, Bob
Durbin, Leo
Duxbury, Frank
Dye, Glen
Edelen, Art
Edelen, Art
Edelen, Bill
Edelen, Bud
Edelen, Doc
Edelen, Jessie
Edelen, Jim
Edmonds, Gil
Edmondson, Rill
Edwards, Scatter
Egan, Bill Governor
Egan, Truk
Elgin, Walter
Ellard, Blackie
Ellie, Ton

Elliott, Al
Elliott, Dick
Ellis, Bill
Ellis, Blackie
Ellis, Linn
Ellis, Sourdough
Ellison, E.R.
Enoch, Joe
Erickson, Dick
Ericson, Dick
Evans, Dave
Evans, Holly
Fairchield, Chuck
Farless, Janus
Farmer, Walt
Farron, Glen
Fenton, Jim
Figlinski, Frank
Fimpel, Hal
Fimpel, Jim
Fine, Larry
Firestone, Bud
Fisher, Brad
Fisher, Doug
Fisher, Gary
Fisher, Terry
Fisher,Bob
Fleur, Martin
Flood, Dave
Flowers, Bob
Floyd, A.J.
Floyd, Andrew
Floyd, Kevin
Ford, Bill
Ford, Ed
Forecheski,J ohn
Foreman, Hank
Foster, Clay
Foster, D.R.
Foster, E.R.
Foster, Jack
Foster, Larry
Fowler, Gene
Fowler, Jim
Frank, D.L.
Frankford, Sam

Franklin, Bob
Franklyn, Sam
Freeman, George
Freeny, John
French, Ted
Fry, Les
Fry, Marvin
Fuller, Jerry
Fulton, Jerry
Gagnon, Paul
Gallager, Bob
Gallager, Bud
Gallop, Freddy
Gardner, Dinnis
Garner, Gene
Garrett, Nelson
Garrison, Jack
Gates, Bill
Gates, Richard
Gay, Ron
Gay, Tom
Gentry, Elmer
Ghan, Blaine
Ghan, Carl
Ghezzi, Al
Giammalva, Joe
Gibson, Don
Gibson, John
Gibson, Richard
Gibson, Sam
Gierman, Tim
Gierman, Tim Jr.
Giglione, Angila
Gilbert, Jim
Gilbert, Tim
Gilbertson, Don
Gilbertson, Joe
Gillick, Al
Gilman, Stan
Gilstrap, Wally
Glaves, Robert
Glaze, Marvin
Glenn, John
Glison, Terry
Gobel, George
Goddard, Jack

Golden, Larry
Goodrich, Bill
Goodrich, Joe
Gordon, Dock
Gordon, Rich
Graham, Bob
Grant, Bob
Grant, Wayne
Graves, Jim
Green, Cliff
Green, Dale
Green, Earl
Green, Jack
Green, Jerry
Green, Lauren
Gregory, Whitey
Grey, Art
Grey, Dick
Grey, John
Grey, Mel
Grey, Ron
Griffen, Vern
Griffin, Earl
Griffith, Earl
Grimsley, Jerry
Grones, Jim
Growden, Andy
Growden, Bill
Growden, Jim
Gruening, Earnest
Gulawite, Red
Gunther, Jim
Hackey, Keith
Hafer, Loren
Hagan, Jewell
Hagen, Jim
Hagen, Ken
Haggerty, Jack
Haines, Joe
Hale, Dave
Hall, Arman
Hall, Bobby
Hall, Carey
Hall, Charles
Hall, Gene
Hall, Harman

Hall, Tom
Halverson, Wayne
Hammond, Bob
Hammond, Governor Jay
Hampton, Bruce
Hannah, Bill
Hannon, Bob
Hansen, Bill
Hansen, Bob
Hanson, Axel
Hanson, Bud
Hanson, Tim
Harang, Gordon
Hardenbrook, Jim
Hardy, Bert
Hardy, Buddy
Hardy, Leo
Hardy, Rick
Hardy, Ronnie
Harley, Kelly
Harper, Niel
Harran, Bill
Harrel, Bob
Harrel, Don
Harris, Jim
Harris, Jim
Harris, Kieth
Harris, M.C.
Harris, Roger
Hart, Dean
Hart, Harold
Hart, Jack
Hartman, Boyd
Hartman, Floyd
Hartman, George
Hartman, Jess
Hartman, Lloyd
Hartman, Roy
Hartman, Wayne
Hayden, J.B.
Hayes, Jim
Hazellief, Donald
Heard, Bob
Heard, Vern
Heart, Harold
Heath, Fred

Heatherly, George
Heatherly, Glen
Hegman, Dick
Hemphil, Roy
Hemphill, Al
Hemphill, Ray
Hendrickson, Chuck
Hensley, Steve
Herda, Al
Herfendahl, ?
Herring, Art
Herring, Don
Hess, Tom
Hickman, Don
Hidebrand, Bud
Higginbothm, John
Hightower, Bill
Hildebrand, Bob
Hill, Bob
Hill, Cliff
Hill, Donny
Hill, Mike
Hillar, George
Hinkle, Larry
Hinman, Tom
Hite, Tommy
Hoagland, Dale
Hoeman, Del
Hoff, Vern
Holden, Curt
Holland, Jim
Holland, Virgil
Hood, Bill
Hood, Dick
Hood, Erin
Hood, Johnn
Hopkins, Ron
Hoskins, Vic
Howard, Bob
Howard, Jim
Howell, Merve
Hoyt, Craig
Hoyt, Fred
Hubbard, Richard
Hubbard, Rusty
Huff, Gary

Huffman, Gary
Huffman, George
Huffman, Jim
Huntly, Gene
Hupprich, Fred
Hurd, Bob
Hurd, Vern
Huston, Don
Huston, Lee
Isacson, Ike
Jackson, Action
Jackson, Dexter
Jackson, Stan
James, Bill
James, Fred
James, Jerry (Wildman)
James, Kenny
James, Mike
Jansen, Harold
Jansen, Ken
Jansen, Paul
Jansen, Vic
Jarvey, Abe
Jeffries, Jerry
Jeffries, Paul
Jensen, Al
Jensen, Hank
Jensen, J.J.
Jewel, Walter
Jewel, Wilburn
Johnson, Andy
Johnson, Arron
Johnson, Bill
Johnson, Dan
Johnson, Dick
Johnson, Fred
Johnson, Glen
Johnson, Hambone
Johnson, Hap
Johnson, Hilmer
Johnson, Jack
Johnson, Jeff
Johnson, Jim
Johnson, John
Johnson, John
Johnson, Lawrence

Johnson, Lyle
Johnson, Mark
Johnson, Nic
Johnson, Pat
Johnson, Warren
Johnson, Wayne
Johnston, Lyle
Jones, Al
Jones, Bob
Jones, Gary
Jones, Jerry
Jones, Jim
Jones, Ken
Jordan, Orville
Joyce, Bill
Karman, Wilber
Kearns, Ed
Keeler, Ed
Keller, Fred
Kelly, Bev
Kelly, Mason
Kelly, Pat
Kelly, Ron
Kemp, Si
Kennedy, D.T.
Kent, Don
Kent, Gene
Kent, Harold
Kern, Ed
Kerns, Robert
Kettish, Len
Kiehl, Glenn
Kiester, Blackie
Kiester, Jack
Kildahl, Paul (Piano)
Killion, Maurice
Kinchey, Ken
Kincy, Dean
Kindley, Jerry
Kindly, Jimmy
King, Butch
King, Casey
King, Ed
King, Edwin
King, Michael
King, Wayne

Kirby, Jim
Kirkpatrick, Max
Klien, Ralph
Knight, Bill
Knight, Dick
Knight, Gil
Knoll, Clarence
Knudsen, Jerry
Knudson, John
Knudson, Ted
Koegle, Otto
Kok, Glen
Kopf, Bernard
Kraft, Dennis
Kramer, George
Kriner, Park
Kroger, Otto
Krukenberg, Ray
Kukenberg, Rich
La Bonte, Lewis
Labey, Dan
Labonte, Lewis
LaCross, Jack
Laird, Dan
Lake, Kelly
Lake, Orville
Lambert, Troy
Lance, Doug
Landry, Larry
Lane, Jim
Lane, Ron
Langford, Steve
Langley, Rich
Lanning, Dave
Lappka, Leon
Larkin, Ray
Larson, George
Larson, Ken
Larson, Lud
Larson, Mike
Lasko, Ted (Pickles)
Lathrop, Clarence
LaTorre, Joe
Lavery, Bill (pilot)
Lawrence, Tiny
Lawrence, Tommy

Leaf, Daniel
Leary, Jack
LeBrell, Kim
LeBrell, Mark
Lee, Al
Lee, Bob
Lee, J.C.
Lee, Oscar
Leggo, Bruce
Leland, Lee
Lemaire, Dave
Lemmon, Bill
Leslie, Jim
Lewis, Allan
Liddington, Dan
Lindquist, Steve
Little, Carl
Little, Needa
Little, Ron
Little, Sam
Lloyd, Dale
Lofgren, Wayne
Long, Bill
Long, Dan La
Lounsberry, David
Lounsbury, George
Lounsbury, Lloyd
Lowery, Ken
Lund, Jim
Luther, Ed
M'Ginn, John
MacDonald, Harry
MacDonald, John
Madson, Ken
Magee, Terry
Malcomb, Don
Mangonelli, Art
Mann, Wayne
Marinoski, Bill
Marquiss, Bud
Martin, Bill
Martin, Dean
Martin, Don
Martin, John
Martin, Steve
Martin, Vern

Martinez, Mike
Masher, Glen
Maskal, Bob
Matlock, Matt
Matlock, Nat
Mattheusin, Ken
Matthews, Bob
Matthews, Jim
Mattingly, Dennis
Mattingly, Matt
Maxwell, bob
Maybry, Lloy
McCahill, Tom
McClanahan, rock
McCleene, Harold
McClure, Earl
McClure. Pat
McCorrmick, John
McCoullugh, Robert
McCurne, Mike
McDonajd, Robert
McDonald, Archie
McDonald, Bill
McDonald, Bob
McDonald, Harry
McDonald, John
Mcdonard, Ben
McDow, Paul
McEnallay, Bill
McFarland, Bill
Mcgee, Bob
Mcgee, Bud
McGee, Bud
McGee, Terry
McGee, Wilbur
McGinley, Frank
McGinley, Philis
Mcintosh, Bob
McKay, Russ
McKee, Charles
McKee, Mack
McKenzi, Rich
McKenzi, Tim
McKenzie, Dean
McKenzie, Jim
McKenzie, Spud

McMcomb, Bob
McMillan, Ken
McMillen, Fred (Trapper)
McNutt, Frank
McPherson, John
Meehan, Bill
Meehan, Bob
Meehan., Billy
Meers, Earl
Meier, Bud (Chrome)
Meiers, Bobby
Mendonsa, Mark
Mendonsa, Mark
Merrit, Del
Merryman, Harry
Messenger, Bob
Meyer, Ed
Meyers, Bob
Meyers, Harold
Mill, Bob
Miller, Billy
Miller, Bob
Miller, Carl
Miller, Dale
Miller, Floyd
Miller, James
Miller, Jim
Miller, Jin
Miller, John
Miller, John (Tennessee)
Miller, Kieth
Miller, Lloyd
Miller, Norman
Miller, Pat
Miller, Rick
Miller, William (Bill)
Millicent, John
Mills, Bill
Mills, Carl
Mitchell, Bob
Mitchell, Clarence
Mitchell, Dean
Mitchell, Gary
Mitchell, Jeff
Mitchell, Tim
Mitdhell, Jim

Molinhower, Marvin
Montgomery, Ed
Montpetit, Bill
Moon, Norman
Moore, Larry
Moore, Mark
Moore, Wayne
Morgan, Jim
Morris, Harvey
Morris, Ivy
Morrow, Ron
Morrow, Tom
Morse, Tini
Mosley, Ed
Moss, Barry
Moss, Charley
Mulinex, Paul
Mullenix, Matt
Munsinger, Bill
Murphy, Don
Myles, Bob
Myles, Bob
Nash, Chubby
Nash, Dan
Needameyer, Bill
Needham, Cliff
Neeley, Si
Nehrbas, George
Nelson, Al
Nelson, Ken
Nelson, Larry
Nelson, Tim
Nelson, Tiny
Ness, Orville
Newberry, Ben
Newberry, Bob
Newberry, Stan
Nichols, George
Noel, Oscar
Nolls, Oscar
Noonan, Mike
Nordyke, Curly
Norris, Ivy
Norton, Bill
Norton, Lester (Smokey)
Noyes, Col

O'Leary, Bernard
O'Leary, Bill
O'Leary, George
Obrien, Wilbur
Odell, Jack
Odell, Jess
Ogden, Dave
Olds, Monte
Oleary, Donny
OLeary, Eddie
Oleary, Howard
Oleary, Jim
Oleary, Morris
Olin, Jerry
Olsen, Harold
Olson, Al
Olson, Curt
Olson, Derrick
Olson, Don
Olson, Frank
Olson, H. W. (Sweed)
Olson, Harold
Olson, Jim
Olson, Ken
Olson, Shorty
Olson, Tim
Oneal, Don
Orcutt, Leonard
Osborn, Warren
Osborne, Emory
Osborne, Hank
Otley, Harold
Ouellrtte, Charles
Painter, Roger
Painter, Russ
Palin, Jim
Palmer, Ray
Parker, Harry
Parker, Harry
Parker, Nick
Parker, Wayne
Partks, Dan
Partrich, Dean
Patterson, Dan
Patterson, Don
Patterson, Willie

213

Paustian, Clyde
Paxson, Ray
Peabody, Mac
Pederson, Anton
Pellicudas, Chris
Pellitier, Jerry
Penny, Jack
People, James
Perkins, Dan
Persinger, Jim
Peters, Rick
Petersn, Albert
Peterson, Duane
Peterson, Pete
Petrovitch, Alex
Petrovitch, George
Petrovitch, Pete
Petty, Jim
Pew, Walt
Phelps, Bud
Phillios, Ray
Phillips, Dennis
Phillips, Larry
Phillips, Ray
Phillips, Vernon
Phipps, Jim
Pierce, Al
Pierce, Doug
Pierce, Eddie
Pierce, Gary
Pierce, Jerry
Pierce, Joe
Pierre, William
Pierson, Ken
Pine, Earl
Pine, Larry
Pine, Ralph
Pineo, Dr. Jim
Pineo, Fred
Plaster, Harold
Playle, James
Porter, Charley
Poston, Posty
Powell, Bod
Powell, Charles
Prall, Kennith

Prince, David
Prince, Dayton
Probert, Al
Probert, George
Profit, Lee
Querrey, Don
Rader, Lowell
Radke, Clarence
Rankin, F.D.
Rankin, W.F.
Rasley, Jim
Rawson, Jack
Ray, Dick
Reed, Art
Reed, Art
Regan, Lance
Renk, Al
Reynolds, John
Rich, R. L.
Richards, Fred (Pard)
Richmond, Jim
Ridder, Kenny
Riechart, John
Rikeman, Bill
Ritche, Al
Rivers, Dick
Rivers, Ken
Rivers, Ralph
Robbins, Ed
Robbins, Pat
Roberts, Bob
Roberts, Bud
Roberts, Dick
Roberts, Ellis
Roberts, John
Robin, Ed.
Rogee, Gene
Rogers, Bill
Rogers, Cal
Rogers, Duane
Rogers, Roy
Rogge, Bill
Rogge, Larry
Rooth, Gunner
Rose, Bill
Rose, Bob

Rosent, Bill
Rosent, Elinore
Ross, Paul
Roundtree, Melvin
Rowe, Dennis
Rowe, R. H.
Rucker, Burl
Rucker, Merle
Rudd, Kieth
Ruddy, Steve
Rudland, Bob
Ruff, Shawn
Ruff, Victor
Rule, Ben
Russel, Bruce
Russel, Cliff
Russel, Jim
Rust, Butch
Rydell, Bob
Sagar, Hubert 'Corky'
Sagar, Hubert 'Pal'
Sallie, John
Sampson, Sam
Sanders, Kieth
Sanders, Ralph
Sanford, Arnold
Sanford, Dale
Sanford, James
Sant, Harold
Sauers, Jack
Saunders, Steve
Schaffer, Jim
Schaffer, Red
Schamberger, roy
Schlotfeldt, Leo
Schmidlkofer, Steve
Schock, Dick
Schook, Tom
Schriener, Jerry
Schroder, Vern
Schrum, Kennith
Schultz, Bud
Schultz, Dave
Schultz, Rich
Scoby, Mable
Scoby, Ray

Scott, Dick
Scott, Harold
Scott, Harold
Scott, RG.
Scrubbs, Bob
Seavers, Les
Sennet, Bobby
Sennet, Lew
Shafer, Jim
Shanks, John
Shannon, Bill
Shannon, Marvin
Shannon, Red
Shaw, Pete
Sheldon, Bobby
Sheldon, Don
Shell, Jim
Shelton, Bill
Sheppard, Ken
Shewa, Warren
Shivers, Sak
Shock, Dave
Shockley, Claude
Shockly, Clyde
Shydler, Mik
Siebenthaler, John
Sievers, Les
Sill, Art
Simmans, Luther
Simmons, Bill
Simmons, Charles
Simpson, Kieth
Sinclair, Ace
Singleton, Don
Sipes, Cecil
Sisson, Jack
Slimsick, Al
Slydel, John
Smart, Clarence
Smart, Vern
Smith, Ed (Pretty Boy)
Smith, George
Smith, Jim
Smith, Max
Smith, Mike
Smith, Ray

Smith, Roy
Smith, Wendel
Smyth,Tom
Sneed, Jim
Sneed, John
Snow, Bob
Snyder, Ray
Sorrows, Slim
Souer, Sam
Spangler, Dan
Spangler, Danny
Sparks, Lotti
Sparks, Paul
Sparling, Dave
Spaulding, Joe
Spears, George
Specking, Keith
Springer, Glen
Springer, Jack
Spurgon, Bud
Staines, Glen
Starkweither, Bill
Starn, Glen
Starnes, Glen
Starnes, Kevin
Starr, Lloud
Starr, Roy
Stater, Don
Statz, Red
Steadman, Cliff
Steadman, Clive
Steel, Allan
Steel, Donald
Steel, Ed
Steele, Jack
Stephens, Al.
Stephens, Art
Stephens, Joe
Stepp, Jim
Sterns, lwonard
Stewart, Doug
Stewart, Jim
Stineman, Bob
Stout, Virgel
Strahl, Robert
Stratton, Bob

Strickland, Fermin
Strome, Hank
Strunk, Ed Pardner
Strunk, Steph
Sturgeon, Bill
Suess, Auggie
Sullivan, George
Sullivan, Jim
Sundt, Arny
Swafford, Tom
Swanson, Jim
Swartz, Steve
Swartz, Tony
Swartzenberger, Bill
Swartzinberger, Joe
Swensen, Evan
Sylvester, Mason
Tabor, Harold
Taft, Everett
Tanahill, Bill
Tannahill, Phil
Tatchick, Charley
Tate, Bob
Tate, Jack
Tate, Walter
Tatlow, Carl
Tatrow, Hugh
Taylor, John
Taylor, Larry
Taylor, Vern
Teague, Frank
Tegler, Meritt
Tempest, Don
Tennison, Curly
Thomas, Gene
Thomas, Ray
Thomes, Wade
Thompson, Doug
Thompson, Doug
Thompson, Grant
Thompson, Loran
Thompson, Mike
Thompson, Warren
Thornton, Burligh
Thornton, Rich
Thrasher, T J.

Thronson, Frank
Tidwell, Shane
Tiech, Bob
Tillinghast, Howard
Tok, Bubbles AT
Tollman Jerrry
Tollman, Ed
Tordoff, Dirk
Tripp, Al
Tripp, George
Tripp, Larry
Tripp, Lee
Tripp, Ron
Tufford, Bill
Tyrell, Ted
Unfer, Bill
Unfer, Vic
Ursick, Rob
Van Avery, Harold
Varner, Bill
Vehmeir, Bill
Veillon, Jacques
Verde, Chico Val
Vincent, Doug
Wade, Buck
Wade, Harry
Wade, Jerry
Wagner, Howard
Wagner, Larry
Waldo, Floyd
Waldon, Bob
Walker, Ed
Walker, Jack
Wallace, Jack
Wallace, Paul
Wallace, Tom
Ward, Bill
Ward, Denny
Ward, Kenny
Warden, Rick
Ware, Steve
Warner, Wayne
Warren, Dennis
Warwick, Andy
Waters, John
Watkins, Bill

Watson, Bill
Watson, Floyd
Watts, John
Weaver, Howard
Weaver, Ken
Weaver, Pat
Weaver, Russel
Weaver, Sam
Webb, Earnest
Webb, Rick
Webster, Ted
Weeks, Lewis
Weeks, Paul
Weeks, Rick
Weeks, Skip
Weeks, Wilbur
Wells, Fuzzy
Wendt, Monte
Wenger, Jack
Werner, Buz
West, Dave
West, Frank
West, Jim
West, Woody
Westfall, Eugene
Wheeler, Pat
White, Frank
White, Tim
Whitford, Buck
Whitford, Norm
Wicken, Ed
Widdington, A.J.
Widington, Martin
Wiger, Walt
Wigman, Bob
Wilbanks, Leonard
Wilcox, Bruce
Wilcox, Dan
Wilcox, Don
Wiley, Pete
Wilhams, Clayton
Wilhelm, Chuck
Wilhite, Sam
Wilke, Ted
Wilkenson, Don
Wilkenson, John

Wilkerson, Charles
Wilkins, Ted
Willfer, Chuck
Willford, Buck
Williams, Bud
Williams, Dan
Williams, Layton
Williams, Leonard
Williams, Martin
Williams, Pat
Williams, Rick
Williams, Russ
Williams, Slim
Willits, Jim
Wilson, Dewayne
Wilson, Paul
Winn, Lee
Winn, Steve
Winter, Wayne
Wold, Sig
Wolf, Gary
Wolf, Gordy
Wood, Art
Wood, Arthur
Wood, Don
Wood, John
Wood, Lymon
Woodford, Harold
Woolward, Harold
Work, Elmer
Workman, Fred
Wright, Dick
Wright, Forest (Punk)
Wright, Tex
Wymiller, Jim
Yelli, Terry
Young, Al
Young, Frank
Young, J.C.
Young, Tom
Younger, John
Zender, Dick
Ziegler, Bob
Zimmerman, Tony
Zolomski, Larry

Appendix B
Alaskan Drivers' and Old-Timers' Photographs

Joe Goodrich and Bob Messenger

Buz Werner

Hoagy Barite and Andy Growden

Otto Koegle

Harold Plaster

Tiny Lawrence, Devera Metzger,
and Ted Chix

Jerry Brosti and Charlie Barr

Clyde Paustian

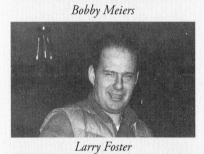

Bobby Meiers

Larry Foster

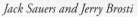

Jack Sauers and Jerry Brosti

Buz Werner

Don Nash and Vic Unfer

Ted Knutson, Don Kuhn, Hoagy
Barite, and Andy Growden

Bill Burnison

Johnny Johnson

*Mel Buck, Lester Norton,
and Freddie (janitor)*

Crazy Christy

Joe Gilbertson and Bill Edwards

Dick Ray

Lester Norton

Bill Hightower

Bill Hood and Ike Isacson

Ted Chix

Ben Rule, Glenn Kiehl,
and Don Singleton

Bob Cavallero and Howard Weaver

Jack Steele and Glenn Bohanon

Bud Meier and Lester Norton

Monte Olds

Tiny Lawrence

Warren Shewa and Glenn Johnson

Bob Howard and Joe Gilbertson

Nick Nichols

Appendix C
Alaska Trucking Companies

Air Land Express
Al Renk and Sons
Alaska Direct
Alaska Freight Lines
Alaska Transfer
Alaska Transport
Alaska West Express
ANCO
Arctic Motor Freight
Aurora Dist.
B.M.R. Trucking
Bayless and Roberts Inc.
Big State Logistics
Big Wheels Trucking
Bishop Trucking Inc.
Bob McComb Trucking
Black Gold
Burk Trucking
Carlyle Trucking
Cat Trucking
City Express
Columbus Dist.
Consolidated Freightways
Copper Freightlines
Curt Trucking
Denali Transportation
Doyle Trucking

Drilling Mud Haulers
Eggor Trucking
Fairbanks Anchorage Xpress
Fairbanks-Anchorage-
Seattle-Transport (FAST)
Femmer Transfer
Frank Figlinski Trucking
Frontier Transportation
Garrison Fast Freight
GNATS
Goldstreak
Heatherly Trucking
Herda Alaska Truck Lines
Hill & Hill
Homer Freightlines
Hoyt Transfer
Irish Trucking
Jims Express Truck Lines
K & W
Kaps Trucking
Kodiak Oilfield Haulers
Larry Reed Truck Service
Lynden Transfer Inc.
Mammoth Truck Lines
Midnight Sun Transportation
Mitchell Truck and Tractor
Millwood Transit Movers Inc.

Movers Inc.
Mukluk
North Pacific Trucking
Northwest Freight Lines
O'Leary & Jewel Trucking
Olson Trucking
Otley Trucking
Pacific West
Peninsula Fast Freight
Pioneer Alaska Express
Polar Roller Express
Portage Transport
R-Dees Alaska
Sagar Trucking
Sea Land
Sig Wold Transfer & Storage
Sourdough Freight Lines
Stallings Truck Lines
Tabor and Rice
Tommy Hite trucking
Unfer Bros.
United Buckingham
V. D. Barber and Sons
Weaver Bros.
Wells Cargo
Wrightway Auto Carriers

Appendix D
Alaska Old-Time Roadhouses

Sterling Highway from Homer to the Seward Highway
Clam Gulch Inn, Kasilof River Inn, Hamilton's at Cooper Landing, Hinton's Lodge at the Ferry, Naptown Inn, Point of View at Cooper Landing, Standard Oil Station at Sterling, Sunset Inn at Kenai Lake.

Seward Highway from Seward to Anchorage
Blondie's at Portage, Fork and Spoon, Anchorage, Jockey Club at Moose Pass, Peggy's, Anchorage.

Glenn Highway from Anchorage to Glennallen
Copper Kettle near King Mountain, Eureka Lodge, King Mountain Café, Long Rifle at Matanuska Glacier, McGinley's Café at Nelchina, Red's Truck Stop, Sutton Roadhouse.

Glennallen
Rosent's Truck Stop.

Glennallen, Richardson Highway, Valdez to Fairbanks
Rickas Roadhouse, Sullivans Roadhouse, 101 Café and Truck Stop Copper Center, 35 Mile Lodge, Tonsina Lodge, Bert & Mary's at Black Rapids, Buffalo Lodge, Delta Junction, Copper Center Lodge, Donnely Inn, Evergreen Lodge, Bay Hotel, Delta Junction, Glennallen Lodge, Lappis Junction Inn at Tok Cutoff and Richardson Highway, Paxson Lodge, Richardson Roadhouse at Delta Jct., Sourdough Lodge at Sourdough River, Summit Lake Lodge, Tekel Lodge, near Thompson Pass.

Tok Cutoff Glennallen to Tok

Bear Cub Lodge, Duffy's, Gakona Lodge, Mentasta Lodge, Molly Persinger's Lodge near Mentasta on old road, past Mineral Lakes, Parker House, Tok.

Alcan Highway, Border to Delta Junction,

Dot Lake Lodge, Forty-Mile Roadhouse, Old Hotel at Scotty Creek, Rose's Truck Stop Café, Scotty Creek Lodge, Tok Tesoro,

Fairbanks

Sunset Strip, Hilltop Truck Stop.

Dalton Highway

Coldfoot Services, mile 175.